# THE EXISTENTIAL RISK

# OF TECHNOLOGY:

# THE DEATH OF

# OUR HUMANITY

# THE EXISTENTIAL RISK OF TECHNOLOGY: THE DEATH OF OUR HUMANITY

## RECLAIMING VALUE, INTIMACY, AND OUTRAGEOUS LOVE IN THE DIGITAL AGE

### FROM ALGORITHMIC ALIENATION TO THE EVOLUTION OF INTIMACY

*One Mountain, Many Paths: Oral Essays*
*Volume 18*

DR. MARC GAFNI

Copyright © 2025 Center for World Philosophy and Religion

All Rights Reserved

No part of this book may be used or reproduced in any manner whatsoever without written permission except in the case of brief quotations embodied in critical articles or reviews.

No part of this book may be reproduced, or stored in a retrieval system, or transmitted in any form or by any means, electronic, mechanical, photocopying, recording, or otherwise, without express written permission of the publisher.

All brand names and product names used in this book are trademarks, registered trademarks, or trade names of their respective holders.

For additional information and press releases please contact CWPR Publishing.

Authors: Marc Gafni
Title: The Existential Risk of Technology
Identifiers: ISBN 979-8-88834-023-3 (electronic)
ISBN 979-8-88834-022-6 (paperback)

© 2025 Marc Gafni

Edited by Elena Maslova-Levin, Talya Bloom, and Rachel Keune

World Philosophy and Religion Press,
St Johnsbury, VT

in conjunction with

**IP** Integral Publishers

https://worldphilosophyandreligion.org

# CONTENTS

EDITORIAL NOTE ABOUT AUTHORSHIP, EDITING,
AND THE RADICAL CONTEXT FOR THIS SERIES                XIV

LOVE OR DIE: LOCATING OURSELVES                        XXIV

ABOUT THIS VOLUME                                      XL

CHAPTER 1    SURVEILLANCE CAPITALISM: "WE'RE GOING
             TO STEAL YOUR EXPERIENCE WITHOUT
             YOUR PERMISSION"

First Principles and First Values Account for the Critiques
  of Natural Law and Perennial Philosophy                1
Mistaken Assumptions of Natural Law and Perennial Philosophy    3
Critiques by Postmodernity of Natural Law and Perennial Philosophy    4
Postmodernity's Critique of Perennialism and Natural Law Is True but
  Partial, and It Ignores Responsibility to Any Larger Grand Narrative—
  Except the Success Story                             5
The Nervous System of the Planet Is the Web, the Worldwide Virtual World    6
Google's Business Model Is Surveillance Capitalism    7
Facebook Hijacks Your Attention, Takes Your Information and Targets You
  With Ads, Thereby Compromising the Free Movement of
  Economy and Governance                               8
We Are Unaware of the Threat to Universal Human Rights    8
The Failure to Articulate the Case Against the Tech Plex Is Rooted in
  a Failure of First Principles and First Values       10
Surveillance Capitalism: We're Going to Steal Your Experience
  Without Your Permission                              12
The Six Declarations of Google                         13

| | |
|---|---|
| Instead of Solving Existential and Catastrophic Risk, Our Best Minds Are Caught in the Success Story | 15 |
| From Holdables to Wearables to Biometric Sensors | 16 |
| First Principles and First Values Refute Surveillance Capitalism | 18 |
| Exposing the Inner Structure in Which Human Experience Is Being Stolen | 20 |
| The Direct, First-Person Experience of Reality Coming Alive in Me | 21 |

## CHAPTER 2  DIAGNOSING THE TECH PLEX: FROM DIGITAL DICTATORSHIP TO DIGITAL INTIMACY, FROM SOCIAL SELF TO UNIQUE SELF, FROM SOCIAL HIVE TO UNIQUE SELF SYMPHONIES

| | |
|---|---|
| Evolutionary Love Code: The Unique Self Is Under Attack by the Tech Plex | 25 |
| The Articulation of Unique Self Consciousness Is the Overriding Moral Imperative of This Generation | 26 |
| Separate Self, Social Self, True Self, and Unique Self | 26 |
| I Am Irreducibly Valuable As a Unique Emergent of the Whole | 27 |
| Your Unique Self Is Your Unique Response-Ability to Reality | 28 |
| Your Unique Self Has Irreducible Value | 29 |
| B.F. Skinner: The Human Being Is a Social Self | 30 |
| B.F. Skinner: Let's Nullify the Autonomous Man, the Inner Man | 31 |
| Skinner's Approach—Nullifying the Autonomous Man—Is the Basis of Social Media | 32 |
| C.S. Lewis vs. B.F. Skinner: The Abolition of Man, the Abolition of Human Society | 34 |
| However Misguided, Skinner Is Responding to Existential Risk and Critiquing Separate Self As the Source of Human Dignity | 37 |
| Skinner Did Not Have the Tools to Develop Technologies of Human Behavior | 38 |
| Alex Pentland, One of the Architects of the Web, Is a Direct Continuation of Skinner | 39 |
| Pentland: Data Science Is the New Physics Which Will Allow Us to Enact a New Vision of Society | 41 |

| | |
|---|---|
| The Founders of the Tech Plex Adopt the Vision of Skinner and Pentland | 41 |
| Social Media Is an Expression of Skinner's Walden Two | 42 |
| We Need to Replace the Understanding of Natural Law With Evolving Perennialism, an Evolving Set of First Values and First Principles | 43 |
| The Tech Plex: We Are Organizing Society as Social Selves | 44 |
| True Self and Unique Self Are Ignored by the Tech Plex | 45 |
| Unseen, Pentland and Skinner Have Formed the Thinking of the Tech Plex, Which Arrogates to Itself the Right to Your Experience | 46 |
| Personal Data Is Currently Being Used by Machine Intelligence Algorithms to Compromise the Two Basic Identities of Democracy: the Voter and the Consumer | 47 |
| Under-The-Skin Surveillance Is the Next Step and Will Result in Digital Dictatorships | 47 |
| The Postmodern Deconstruction of Value Together With Surveillance Capitalism Results in the "Conditioners" Predicted by C.S. Lewis | 48 |
| We Need to Respond to Social Self With Unique Self | 49 |
| The Power and Profit Agenda Together With Utopianism, Sans First Principles and First Values | 50 |
| Imagine What Happens When a Dictatorship Owns Data | 51 |
| In the Absence of Unique Self, Social Self Became the Animating Energy of the Nervous System of the Planet | 52 |
| Our Job Is to Engage in a Reconstructive Project of Value so We Can Muster the Necessary Outrage Against the Tech Plex | 53 |

**CHAPTER 3　THE NEW EXISTENTIAL RISK: NOT THE DEATH OF HUMANITY BUT THE DEATH OF OUR HUMANITY— THE DEHUMANIZING CREEP OF MACHINE INTELLIGENCE**

| | |
|---|---|
| We're Here to Tell the New Story | 56 |
| Existential Risk: The End of Humanity | 58 |
| Existential Risk Due to Rivalrous Conflict | 59 |

We Need a New Story of Value Grounded in
First Principles and First Values — 59

Articulation of a Second Form of Existential Risk:
The Death of Our Humanity — 61

Living Within the Tao — 68

It's Not That We Become Bad Human Beings,
but That We Cease Being Human — 69

The Quality of Your Unique Voice Is Sacred — 71

Evolutionary Love Code: You Are a Unique Self — 73

Deep Inwardness Is Where We Create Meaning — 75

## CHAPTER 4  THE UNIQUE SELF RESPONSE TO THE EXISTENTIAL RISK OF THE TECH PLEX

The Human Being As a Unique Configuration of Evolutionary Love — 78

Recoding the Algorithmic Structure of the Nervous System of the Planet — 81

Evolutionary Love Code: Unique Voice, Prayer, and the Tech Plex — 82

A Revolution of Self: Re-"Self"ing — 87

## CHAPTER 5  RE-SELFING THE HEART OF THE COSMOS: ACTIVATING UNIQUE SELF AND UNIQUE SELF SYMPHONIES

We Are a Band of Outrageous Lovers, Revolutionaries Who
Are Evolving the Source Code of Culture — 90

We Need a New Story of Value, Grounded in
First Principles and First Values — 94

Evolutionary Love Code: The Unique Self Is the Inward Space of Uniquely
Lived Experience From Which Meaning Is Discovered — 96

The First Principles and First Values of Prayer — 98

**CHAPTER 6    GOD NEEDS YOUR SERVICE: THE GREAT DIVINE RISK, THE FIRST PRINCIPLE OF UNIQUE SELF**

The Choice Is Ours: We Can Either Destroy Ourselves or
   Become a Model for Life in the Galaxy     103

The Story of Humanity Is God's Great Risk     105

Evolutionary Love Code: Your Unique Gift Addresses a Unique Need     107

First Principles and First Values of Cosmos:
   Three Primordial Perspectives     109

**CHAPTER 7    FROM THE HUMILIATION OF NEED TO "YOUR NEED IS MY ALLUREMENT"**

Setting Our Intention: Recoding the Source
   Code in Order to Be at Home in Reality     112

Our Deepest Experience of Love Points to
   The Experience of Cosmos With Itself     114

Evolutionary Love Code: If You Ask, You Must
   Surely Need—Your Need Is My Allurement     115

Cosmos Is a Love Story, and
   Love Always Responds to Genuine Need     116

In Prayer, God Says, "Your Need Is My Allurement"     117

The Practice: Prayer Is Always in Some Way
   Held and Heard and Responded to     119

"Your Need Is My Allurement" Restores the Dignity of Need
   and Eviscerates Shame     119

The Shame in Getting My Needs Met Can Be Healed in the Sexual     121

We Participate in the Allurement of Reality, and When That
   Allurement Is Broken We Have a Desperate Need     123

**EPISODE 228:    IF YOU ASK, YOU MUST SURELY NEED: YOUR NEED IS MY ALLUREMENT**

Setting Our Intention: Humans Are *Homo Imaginus*     125

*Homo amor* Accesses His/Her Unique
   Outrageous Acts Of Love Through Imagination     126

Seeking Intimacy Is a Feature of Reality Evolving Through Us     129

Story: The Baal Shem Tov—"If You Ask, You Must Surely Need"     132

Your Need Is My Allurement     135

## CHAPTER 8    THE TAO THAT CAN BE CODED IS NOT THE TAO: EVOLVING HUMANITY BEYOND ALGORITHMS

Telling a New Story Rooted in Eternal and Evolving Values     137

Evolutionary Love Code: To Think We Have Stepped Out of
the Tao Is the Greatest Existential Risk of All     140

The Tao That Can Be Spoken Is Not the Tao     143

The Death of Our Humanity Begins When We
Think We've Stepped Out of the Tao     145

## CHAPTER 9    YOUR HOLY AND YOUR BROKEN ARE BOTH HALLELUJAH: BEING THE NEW HUMAN IN THE TAO

We Are a Unique Self Symphony, an Emergent Expression of the Tao     147

The Unique Self Symphony in Response to the Tech Plex     149

Imagine a Unique Self Facebook With
7.7 Billion Users Joining Together in Symphony     150

Evolutionary Love Code: The Eternal Tao Is the Evolving Tao     151

Love Is Both Eternal and It Evolves     152

The Tao Is the Realization of the Unquantifiable Value
of a Human Being     153

There's a Shattering in Everything That Reality Has
Made—That's How the Light Gets in     154

Reshimu: Traces of Transcendence     158

## CHAPTER 10    EVOLUTION IS PERSONAL: A SCIENTIFIC TRUTH

We Are Evolution in Person     162

Re-reading Neurochemistry as an Expression of the Intimate Universe     164

In Prayer We Turn to the Infinity of Intimacy That Knows Our Name     167

The Internet Is the Shallows, the Clarified Heart-Mind Expresses Depth     169

## CHATPER 11  THE ARC OF THE INTIMATE UNIVERSE BENDS TOWARD EVOLUTIONARY UNIQUE SELF

| | |
|---|---:|
| Reality Moves Towards More Intimacy, Wholeness, Aliveness, Depth, Ecstasy, and Kindness | 176 |
| The Principles of Revolution: Telling the New Story | 177 |
| All of Reality Is Intimate, All the Way Up and All the Way Down | 179 |
| The Internet Must Be Recoded From "The Shallows" to Depth and Intimacy | 181 |
| Who Am I? The Separate-Self Narrative | 183 |
| Who Am I? The Social-Self Narrative | 184 |
| Who Am I? The Unique-Self Narrative | 187 |
| Social Self: Rats in the Maze of the Tech Plex | 188 |
| Unique Self as Part of a Symphony | 189 |

## CHAPTER 12  THE GOOD NEWS: HOMO AMOR, WE ARE ALL NEEDED

| | |
|---|---:|
| The Dangers of Inaccurate, Partial Stories | 193 |
| Reclaiming the Evangelical Spark That Has Been Hijacked | 195 |
| To Be an Evangelist Is to Be an Outrageous Lover | 197 |
| Outrageous Love: We're Outraged | 200 |
| Evolutionary Love Code: For True Evangelism We Need Both Ecstatic States and Developmental Stages | 201 |
| In Every Great Tradition There's an Intimate Incarnation of the Divine | 204 |
| Passover: Reclaiming the Broken Part | 205 |

**INDEX**      **210**

# EDITORIAL NOTE ABOUT AUTHORSHIP, EDITING, AND THE RADICAL CONTEXT FOR THIS SERIES

## ORAL ESSAYS FROM THE ONE MOUNTAIN, MANY PATHS WEEKLY BROADCAST

This volume is part of the Oral Essays library, a series of lightly edited, compiled transcripts of oral teachings given by Dr. Marc Gafni and the late Barbara Marx Hubbard in their weekly online broadcast, *One Mountain, Many Paths,* which they co-founded in 2017. Originally called an "Evolutionary Church," *One Mountain, Many Paths* became a key venue for the articulation of an inspired and deeply grounded new Story of Value in response to the meta-crisis. Marc and Barbara—together with Zak Stein,[1] Kristina Kincaid, Ken Wilber, Sally Kempton, Lori Galperin, Aubrey Marcus and dozens of other thought-leaders over the years—began to articulate what they call a World Philosophy and World Religion[2] as a context for our diversity.

---

[1] Zak, together with Ken Wilber, has been Marc's primary intellectual partner and an initiate lineage holder in CosmoErotic Humanism.

[2] This project is grounded in four core organizational frameworks: 1) The Center for World Philosophy and Religion, co-founded by Marc Gafni, Zachary Stein, Sally Kempton, and Ken Wilber, and chaired over the years by John P. Mackey, Barbara Marx Hubbard, Aubrey Marcus, Gabrielle Anwar and Shareef Malnik, Carrie Kish and Adam Bellow, and Kathleen J. Brownback. 2) The Office for the Future, chaired by Stephanie Valcke and Ivan Bossyut. 3) The World Philosophy and Religion Press, founded and chaired by Aubrey Marcus, together with Marc Gafni and Zachary Stein. 4) The Foundation for Conscious Evolution, founded by Barbara Marx Hubbard and currently chaired by Peter Fiekowsky. For a complete list of key leadership, see the Office for the Future website, www.officeforthefuture.com.

## EDITORIAL NOTE

Until Barbara's passing in 2019, she and Marc transmitted teachings together as evolutionary partners and "whole mates," weaving together insights and transmissions from their decades of practice, study, teaching, and activism into a synergy of wisdom, a grounded vision for future policy across all sectors of society.

Much of the *dharma* material below comes directly from Marc, so it was originally all in quotation marks—but that looked a little odd. So per his suggestion we removed them, and the reader should consider the paragraphs on the next several pages as one extended quote from him. We are joyfully grateful to Marc for the clarity of his *dharma*, the elegance and "second simplicity" of this language, and the mad, Outrageous Love with which he transmits his teachings.

Barbara and Marc called the mission of *One Mountain* "a Planetary Awakening in Evolutionary Love Through Unique Self Symphonies." We are an evolutionary community with a deeply grounded, radically alive, and "post-tragic" revolutionary spirit. We are activating a new humanity and awakening as a new species: *Homo amor*, the fulfillment of *Homo sapiens*.

*One Mountain* is committed to articulating a Story of Value that can become the ground for the new society that must be birthed in response to the meta-crisis. We recognize that we are living at a pivotal moment in history. In this "time between stories," the great moral imperative is to tell the new Story of Value. It is ours to do, personally and collectively, with great trembling and ecstatic joy.

## FROM DOGMA TO DHARMA: ETERNAL AND EVOLVING FIRST PRINCIPLES AND FIRST VALUES

The teachings are grounded in decades of deep study across many wisdom traditions. Over the years, week by week, these teachings were incrementally developed within the framework of the *One Mountain, Many Paths* broadcast. We often refer to these teachings as *dharma*.

This word was originally used in lineage traditions to refer to something like universal law. This is a crucial realization: just as there is universal law in mathematical value, there is also a sense of universal law in ethics and value.

Historically, *dharma* often devolved into unchanging dogma. Evolution was ignored, and the natural process of *dharma* evolution became disconnected from its deep, eternal context. The weakness of the word *dharma* is that too often it did not include the evolving insights of the sciences, it confused local cultural truths with universal truths, and it used words like "eternal," as in "eternal Tao," as opposed to words like "evolution."

Eternal came to mean unchanging, and that kind of thinking often led to overly ethnocentric readings of *dharma*. Local systems would claim their religious and cultural insights as immutable, which stood in the way of the emergence of a genuine world Story of Value that is real, inherent to Cosmos, and backed by the Universe—even as it is also always evolving.

Or, as we often say, "eternal value is evolving value. The eternal Tao is the evolving Tao."

We have shown that, emergent from profound insights in the "interior sciences," eternal does not mean unchanging in time; it means what we call the deeper Field of ErosValue that is beneath culture, geography, and history, which lives beneath all individual and collective values, and beneath time and space itself.

As such, we have gradually transitioned from the term *dharma* to the term *Value*, in the sense of the Field of Value that lives beneath all values. This Field of Value discloses as First Principles and First Values embedded in a Story of Value.

Indeed, as the interior sciences knew and the exterior sciences imply, Reality arises in a Field of ErosValue in which an entire set of mathematical, musical, molecular, moral, and mystical values are the very ground of all being. That Field of Value is eternal—the true ground of the Good, True and Beautiful—even as it is evolving.

But of course, it is equally critical not just to talk about evolving value, but to ground the evolving value in its true nature, the eternal Field of First Principles and First Values, always reaching for ever more life, ever more love, ever more care, ever more depth, ever more uniqueness, ever more intimate communion, and ever more transformation.

As such, when we refer to the word *dharma*, which still appears in these texts together with the word value, we refer to an evolving *dharma* grounded in an *eternal and evolving* Field of Value. Indeed, eternity and evolution are two faces of the whole, opposites joined at the hip, that characterize the nature of our Cosmos in virtually all of its expressions.

It's in these terms that we ground a robust world philosophy that integrates the validated, leading-edge insights of premodern traditional wisdom, modern wisdom, and more recent postmodern insights, weaving them together into a new whole greater than the sum of its parts.

This new whole is a shared Story of Value rooted in First Principles and First Values that are both eternal and evolving.

These First Principles and First Values of Cosmos are woven together into a new Story of Value as a context for our diversity, a new Universe Story. This new story gives us the best possible responses we have to the mystery, and to the great questions:

- Who am I? Who are we?
- Where am I? Where are we?
- What should I do? What should we do?

It is only through such a shared Universe Story—a narrative of identity and ethos as a context for our blessed diversity—that we can realize how what unites us is so much greater than what divides us.

# THE EXISTENTIAL RISK OF TECHNOLOGY

Only a new Story of Value will allow us to both respond to the meta-crisis and participate together in birthing the most true, good, and beautiful world that we already know is possible.

## THIS ORAL ESSAYS SERIES IS AN ENTRYWAY TO THE GREAT LIBRARY OF COSMOEROTIC HUMANISM

This Oral Essays series is part of the overarching project of the Great Library at the Center for World Philosophy and Religion, led by Dr. Marc Gafni, together with Dr. Zak Stein. The aim of the Great Library project is to articulate a robust and comprehensive new Story of Value, CosmoErotic Humanism, in the form of dozens of well-researched and extensively footnoted academic works.

Our vision is to provide the philosophical framework that will be vital for navigating humanity through this time of immense crisis and transformation.

To begin your journey into CosmoErotic Humanism, we tenderly refer you to the book *First Principles and First Values*, co-authored by Marc Gafni, Zak Stein, and Ken Wilber, under the name David J. Temple. David J. Temple is a pseudonym created for enabling ongoing collaborative authorship at the Center for World Philosophy and Religion. The two primary authors behind David J. Temple are Marc Gafni and Zak Stein, and for different projects, specific writers will be named as part of the collaboration, such as Ken Wilber and others.

Three other volumes complete this introduction: *A Return to Eros*, by Marc Gafni and Kristina Kincaid; *Your Unique Self*, by Marc Gafni; and *Education in a Time between Worlds*, by Zak Stein.

We hope that the Oral Essays in the present volume, with their informal style of transmission, will serve as an allurement and entryway for you into the more formal books of the Great Library that provide the robust intellectual underpinnings of the new Story of Value.

## A NOTE ABOUT THE EDITORS

This Oral Essays collection has been edited by students of the new Story of CosmoErotic Humanism. Each of us has actively participated in *One Mountain, Many Paths*, and most of us have been in deep "Holy of Holies" study with Dr. Marc Gafni for many years.

We have been privileged to find ourselves well-versed in the teachings, and even emerging as lineage-holders of CosmoErotic Humanism.[3]

We view this editing project as a privilege and a deep practice of study and clarification. We experience ourselves as a *mystical editing society*, frequently meeting and conversing together about the content—the depth of knowledge and wisdom offered here—as well as the technical intricacies involved with publishing a beautiful and coherent series of books. In so

---

3  CosmoErotic Humanism is a world philosophical movement aimed at reconstructing the collapse of value at the core of global culture. Much like Romanticism or Existentialism, CosmoErotic Humanism is not merely a theory but a movement that changes the very mood of Reality. It is an invitation to participate in evolving the source code of consciousness and culture towards a cosmocentric *ethos* for a planetary civilization.

The term CosmoErotic Humanism, initially coined by Dr. Gafni and colleagues, points to a complex, multi-faceted, layered, and nuanced evolutionary set of insights that has evolved over decades of intensive research, teaching, and spiritual practice from deep within a wide range of wisdom traditions (including the Wisdom of Solomon lineage tradition, Bodhisattva Buddhism, and Kashmir Shaivism), as well as multiple disciplines including complexity theory, chaos theory, emergence theory, molecular biology, and the more classical disciplines of the humanities.

The seeds of CosmoErotic Humanism were planted with Dr. Marc Gafni's work on a two-volume, 1,000-page opus called *Radical Kabbalah* (Integral Publishers, 2012). This scholarly work, sourced from deep study within the esoteric lineage texts of the Wisdom of Solomon, points to a non-dual, or acosmic, realization which—unlike the prevailing conceptualization of non-duality—does not efface the human being; rather, it is highly humanistic in its nature. The next step in the evolution of CosmoErotic Humanism was the insight that all of Reality is evolving Eros, which lives in, as, and through the human being.

A failure of Eros leads inexorably to the creation of narratives of "pseudo-eros." CosmoErotic Humanism is a response to the modern mental and social breakdown sourced in the proliferation of multiple forms of pseudo-eros and its broken narratives, such as rivalrous conflict governed by win/lose metrics and the dogmatic denial of intrinsic value in Cosmos, which together generate our current "global intimacy disorder."

doing, we function as a "Unique Self Symphony," which itself is a Dharmic term that connotes an omni-considerate collaboration between realized Unique Selves synergizing our unique gifts into a new emergence greater than the sum of the parts. Even as we worked diligently to standardize our editing styles, meeting on a weekly basis to debate the nuances of phrasing, we also operated from within a deep appreciation of the unique style that each editor brought to his or her work. As such, the reader might notice some variation in editing style among the books.

Please note that Dr. Marc Gafni has not reviewed these edited Oral Essays, as he is deeply engaged in writing the formal books of the Great Library. But he has been generous in responding to questions and providing overall guidance in the project. Overall, as Marc's students and students of the *dharma*, we have made it a key project at the Center to publish these pieces of work relatively independently.

## OUR UNIQUE ORAL-ESSAY EDITING STYLE PRESERVES THE ENERGY OF THE ORIGINAL TRANSMISSION

Dr. Marc Gafni is a uniquely gifted teacher whose oral transmission is imbued with a quality that has proven transformative for his students. Many of us feel mystically transformed by both the content and the underlying energy of the transmission style. Therefore, as we like to say, *trust the magic ways the dharma comes through your unique understanding!*

As Marc's empowered students, colleagues, and beloved friends, we have a deep knowing that these teachings are vital for the survival and thriving of humanity as we know it, and we recognize the importance of publishing his teachings in a written format that will be accessible by future generations. At the same time, we sought to preserve the Eros of the original oral transmission with all of its nuance, power, and depth. Our intention in the editing process, to the greatest extent possible, has been to keep these spoken artifacts intact in order to maintain the flow of the original transmission. We have therefore chosen not to engage in intensive formal editing, as we found that doing so resulted in the loss of the energetic transmission that is so key to fully receiving the *dharma*.

After experimenting with many ways to present these texts, we developed a specific way of laying out the text on the page. Marc, in collaboration with Zak Stein and Russian intellectual/artist Elena Maslova-Levin—and ultimately all of the editors, through many conversations—developed a unique, artistic presentation of the text, using bolding, italics, bullet points, and other stylistic features which together serve to accentuate the immediacy of the oral transmission.

As part of this editing style, intended to preserve the integrity of the original transmission, we have refrained from removing the frequent recapitulations of key themes. We found that each recapitulation contributes something vital to the rhythm and music beneath the words, like the beating drum of our hearts. These recapitulations not only review previous material but also add important new emphases, perspectives, and elements of the new Story of Value. We ask for your patience as a reader to trust the rhythm of these texts, and we trust you as a reader to have the depth and steadiness to find your way through.

## KEY COMPONENTS: LINK TO THE ORIGINAL BROADCAST, EVOLUTIONARY LOVE CODES AND PRAYER

To supplement the written word, each episode includes a QR code linking to the original broadcast on YouTube, as well as occasional links to featured songs and video clips.

Each episode also centers around an "Evolutionary Love Code," formulated by Marc. These codes are part of the ongoing articulation and distillation of the *dharma* as it unfolds and emerges, week by week, over the course of many years, through the mystical process we call Outrageous Love or Evolutionary Love.

Another core component of the *One Mountain, Many Paths* episodes is what Marc and Barbara called "Evolutionary Prayer." Prayer is experienced in *One Mountain* not in the old fundamentalist sense of a "cosmic vending-machine god" who is alienated from Cosmos. Marc refers to this as the "god you do not and should not believe in"—and he often adds, "the god you don't believe in does not exist."

## GOD IS THE INFINITE INTIMATE

In fact, in the *dharma* of CosmoErotic Humanism, a new name for God has emerged: the "Infinite Intimate," who appears in first-, second-, and third-person expressions. Marc first shared this name as he heard it whispered in 2023, although earlier intimations and formulations of the name appeared as early as 2010.

In first person, God is infinitely alive and as intimate as our own first-person experience.

In second person, God is the infinitely intimate Personhood of Cosmos that knows our name and holds us—the God about whom we say, *whenever we fall, we fall into Her hands*. This is the God who is our Beloved, Father, Mother, Lover, and Evolutionary Partner.

Finally, in third person, God inheres in all of the First Principles and First Values of Cosmos, and in the laws of science (both interior and exterior) that govern manifest Reality.

Therefore, we have a realization of God as not only the Infinity of Power but also the Infinity of Intimacy.

In *One Mountain, Many Paths*, we are reclaiming prayer at a higher level of consciousness. And we are reclaiming prayer as deep, alive, loving, and intimate conversations with God as the Infinite Intimate who knows our name.

## EDITORIAL NOTE

## THE INVITATION

We invite you to find your way into this revolution. Each one of our Unique Selves and unique gifts are desperately needed as we co-create this new Story of Value together, as part of the covenant between generations, for the sake of the whole.

Let's *play a larger game* and evolve the very source code of consciousness and culture together.

With mad love,

The Editors

# LOVE OR DIE

# LOCATING OURSELVES: ARTICULATING THE ESSENTIAL CONTEXT FOR THE ONE MOUNTAIN, MANY PATHS ORAL ESSAYS

### SETTING OUR INTENTION

Intention setting is everything.

**We're here**—as da Vinci was with his cohort in the Renaissance—**to play a larger game, to participate in the evolution of love, which is to tell the new Story of Value rooted in First Principles and First Values.**

- Our intention is to recognize the critical historical juncture in which we find ourselves.
- Our intention is to take our seat at the table of history and to say, *we take responsibility for this.*
- Our intention is to participate as revolutionaries for the sake of the whole.

What we're here to do is revolution; revolution for the sake of the evolution of love.

It's a revolution for the sake of the trillions of unborn lives that will not manifest:

- The unborn loves
- The unborn creativity
- The unborn goodness
- The unborn truth
- The unborn beauty

**All of it looks to us.**

Not because we're engaged in grandiosity. Not at all!

- We're trembling before She.
- We're trembling with joy at the privilege.
- We're trembling with joy at the responsibility.
- We're trembling with joy at the Possibility of Possibility.
- We have to enact a new story in this moment of time. Because it is only a new story that can change the vector of history.

**The most revolutionary act that we can do**—the greatest moral imperative of this time—**is to articulate a new story at this time between worlds and this time between stories.**

Story is not made up, as postmodernity suggests. **We all live in inescapable frameworks; our framework is the story we live in.** Right now, Reality lives according to win/lose metrics, a story that is generating existential risk. **We need to change that story.**

**When we change that story, when we tell a new story**—not a made-up story, but a new Story of Value, rooted in First Principles and First Values—**then it all changes.**

**We need to participate in the evolution of the source code of consciousness and culture, which is the evolution of love.**

It's the most important, exciting, evolutionary, revolutionary act that we can do to alleviate suffering: to be lovers.

Like Rumi, the great poet of Sufism, we have to be "mad lovers," because it's the only sanity.

To be mad lovers is to see around the corner, to not be so obsessed with the details of the contractions of my life.

*Let me see bigger.*

Let me take complete care of myself in every possible way, let me completely attend to those in my circle of intimacy and influence, and then—*let me expand my circle.*

**That's what we're here for.**

- Our intention is to participate in the *LoveForce*, the *LoveIntelligence*, the *LoveBeauty*, the *LoveDesire* that literally animates Cosmos all the way up and all the way down.
- Our intention is to participate in the evolution of love.

*[In the next few pages we will cover some key concepts which are essential to locating ourselves and setting the context for all the One Mountain, Many Paths Oral Essays. —Eds.]*

## OVERVIEW: EROS IS NO LONGER A LUXURY—IT'S LOVE OR DIE

Eros is life.

The failure of Eros destroys life.

Our lack of Eros is poised to destroy the world.

All civilizations have fallen because the stories that they lived in were, in some sense, stories based on rivalrous conflict governed by win/lose metrics. Every civilization was weakened by interior polarization caused by the lack of a shared Story of Value.

We now have a global civilization, but we haven't created a shared Story of Value.

We haven't solved the generator functions that caused all civilizations to fall. Our global civilization has exponential technologies and extraction models depleting the Earth of resources that took billions of years to create, which is going to lead to a civilizational collapse.

Existential risk is risk to our very existence.

---

*The choice is clear: love or die.*

---

It's that simple.

**Eros is no longer a luxury. It is an absolute necessity for the survival of the individual and the planet.**

In the last half a century, modern psychology has documented an age-old truth: a fully nourished baby who is not held in loving arms will die.

So too, our world, both personal and global—even with all the resources of intelligence and technology at our disposal—will die without being held in love, in the embrace of Eros.

**We must embrace a personal path of love and a global politics of love.**

Not ordinary love. Not love which is "mere human sentiment," but Eros, or what we sometimes call Outrageous Love, which is the heart of existence itself.

We live in a world of outrageous pain.

The only response is Outrageous Love.

## WHAT IS EROS?

**Eros is the experience of radical aliveness, moving towards, seeking, desiring ever deeper contact and ever greater wholeness.**[4] Eros is the core fabric of Reality's being and the motivational architecture of Reality's becoming.

Eros is what animates the evolutionary impulse itself, from the very inception of Cosmos all the way to our very selves, who awaken to the realization that the evolutionary impulse throbs uniquely in each of us.

The realization of human awakening and transformation that lies at the core of the interior sciences is the invitation—or even the urgent and desperate demand—of a madly loving Cosmos animated by infinities of power and infinities of intimacy.

The demand—the desperate invitation, the plea, the tender and fierce command of Cosmos that lives inside every human being—is to awaken: to awaken to our true nature as unique incarnations of Eros and Ethos that are needed and desperately desired by All-That-Is. Said slightly differently: Reality is Eros. Or: God is Eros.

**The failure of Eros destroys life.** The collapse of Eros is always the hidden (or not so hidden) root cause for the collapse of ethics.

This is true both personally and collectively. We live in a moment of a worldwide and personal collapse of Eros. Our lack of Eros is poised to destroy

---

[4] We define Eros through what we refer to as the Eros equation (one of a series of what we call interior science equations):

*Eros = Radical Aliveness* x *Desiring (Growing + Seeking)* x *Deeper Contact* x *Greater Wholeness* x *Self Actualization/Self Transcendence (Creation [Destruction])*

There are good reasons for the formal language of the interior science equations in these writings, and the reader is invited to explore them on their own, in particular, in our work, David J. Temple, *First Principles and First Values: Forty-Two Propositions on CosmoErotic Humanism, the Meta-Crisis, and the World to Come* (World Philosophy and Religion, 2024).

the world. Humanity is currently experiencing what has come to be known as existential risk, a risk to our very existence, or what I will refer to as the Second Shock of Existence.

## EXISTENTIAL RISK: THE SECOND SHOCK OF EXISTENCE

**The first shock of existence is the death of the human being—the realization that we will die,** which dawns in human consciousness at the beginning of history. We are not talking about the biological fact of death but the *existential* realization of death. Although the interior sciences disclose that death is a portal between two days (there is vast empirical,[5] philosophical,[6] and anthro-ontological evidence[7] for the continuity of consciousness[8]), death is also, in our own direct surface experience, a stark end. And that is obviously not a bug but a feature in the system.

---

5   We refer to evidence gathered by the most serious of researchers, beginning with Henry and Edith Sedgwick at Cambridge University and William James at Harvard University, and continuing in highly rigorous form for the last 150 years, as recapitulated by Whiteheadian scholar David Ray Griffin in multiple volumes. See also, for example, Dean Radin, *Real Magic: Unlocking Your Natural Psychic Abilities to Create Everyday Miracles* (Potter/TenSpeed/Harmony, 2018), *The Conscious Universe: The Scientific Truth of Psychic Phenomena* (HarperCollins, 2010), and other books. Or see the earlier classic by Frederic William Henry Myers, *Human Personality and Its Survival of Bodily Death* (Longmans, Green, 1907).

6   This requires a cogent analysis of materialism and dualism, and the introduction of the far more cogent third possibility which we have called "pan-interiority."

7   We discuss Anthro-Ontology in some depth in *First Principles and First Values*, and see also the fuller conversation in David J. Temple, *First Principles and First Values: Towards an Evolving Perennialism: Introducing the Anthro-Ontological Method*—both published by World Philosophy and Religion Press, in Conjunction with Integral Publishers. For now, we will simply define it as an "innate and clear interior gnosis directly available to the human being."

8   See Dr. Marc Gafni and Dr. Zachary Stein's essay in preparation, "Beyond Death: Anthro-Ontology, Philosophy, and Empiricism." This essay is slated to appear in the book *Towards a World Religion: Homo Amor Essays*. The essay is also the ground for a larger book by the same authors, *Twelve Portals to Life Beyond Death: Responding to the Second Shock of Existence*, in which we discuss three forms of material: the empirical, the philosophical, and the anthro-ontological, and show how each form discredits the notion of death as the end.

# THE EXISTENTIAL RISK OF TECHNOLOGY

**Our first-person experience is that death ends this life.** It is not the *totality* of our experience if we go deeper inside, but it is obviously intended to be the central, potent, and painful dimension of every human life. Indeed, as Ernest Becker potently reminded us, the denial of death is at our peril.

All the stories and all the plotlines and all the threads of living end at that moment. Whatever happens beyond, we have an actual experience of ending. **Paradoxically, that ending, the experience of the finality of mortality, is what presses us into life.** From the implicit demand of the first shock of existence, human beings were activated and pressed into creative emergence, and what emerged was all of human culture, both interior and exterior.

**The second shock of existence is the realization of the potential death of all humanity.** After all the stages of human history—matter, life, and mind in all of their stages of evolutionary unfolding—we have come to this place in the evolution of humanity, in which the gap between our exponentially expanding exterior technologies and our stalled (or even regressing) interior technologies of value has created dire catastrophic and existential risks.

This gap generates extraction models and exponential growth curves, rivalrous conflicts based on win/lose metrics, tragedies of the commons, and multipolar traps, in which everyone has to keep producing to the $n$th degree, including weaponized exponential threats to our very existence because we are afraid that the other parties are going to do it and not be transparent—hide it from us and then dominate us.

## GENERATOR FUNCTIONS FOR EXISTENTIAL RISK

Let's outline clearly the main *generator functions for existential risk*.

**Rivalrous conflicts governed by zero-sum, win/lose metrics.** Rivalrous conflicts generate extraction models at the core of the economic system and exponential growth curves. Both of these drive and are driven by a contrived system of artificially manufactured desires and needs, delivered into culture by ever more precise forms of micro-targeting to individuals and groups through the ever more immersive environment of the internet.

Next, rivalrous conflicts and exponential growth curves animated by win/lose metrics generate **complicated, fragile world systems** highly vulnerable to myriad forms of collapse. Fragile local systems are made exponentially more fragile on a global level by our inability to meet global challenges with social, legal, political, economic, and ethical infrastructures that remain largely local.

**All of this is a direct result of the failure to develop more adequate interior technologies that would be sufficiently compelling to displace "rivalrous conflict governed by win/lose metrics" as the motivational architecture for the human life world.**

This failure has led to the conditions that will cause the implosion of systems that are already and quite literally on the brink of collapsing themselves. That's what we mean by the *second shock of existence.*

To recapitulate: the second shock of existence is not the death of the human being, but the potential death of humanity.

It is the *Death Star* moment of our species.

## THE DECONSTRUCTION OF INTRINSIC VALUE

We stand in this moment poised between utopia and dystopia, at a time between worlds and a time between stories. We need a new Story of Value, eternal yet evolving, rooted in First Principles and First Values, which would become a universal grammar of value and a context for our diversity.

**This is exactly what the Renaissance was.** It was a time between worlds and a time between stories. In the Renaissance, we had been recently challenged by the Black Death, a pandemic that swept across Europe. The Black Death destroyed between a third to half of Europe and a huge part of

Asia. People died horrifically, brutally, in the streets. They had no idea how to meet this challenge, and so, in response to the Black Death, da Vinci and Ficino and their cohorts understood that they had to tell a new Story of Value.

**That story was the story of modernity. Did they get it right?**

- They got part of it right, which birthed, to use Jürgen Habermas' phrase, "the dignities of modernity," such as new ways of gathering information and universal human rights.
- But they also deconstructed the source of Value. They lost the basis for the Good, the True, and the Beautiful.

The basis used to be divine revelation: *God told us*. But this claim was owned by religion, and every religion began to overreach and over-claim. The revelation was thus often mediated through cultural categories and wasn't fully accurate.

> *Modernity threw out revelation, but was unable to establish a new basis for value.*

**Value was just assumed to be real**. As it says in the founding document of the American Revolution: *We hold these truths to be self-evident*—that is, *we don't really have a basis for value; we just take it as a given.*

**In other words, modernity took out a loan of social capital from the traditional world.** The source of value was never worked out.

**And then, gradually, value began to collapse.**

- The Universe Story began to collapse.
- The belief that the Good, the True, and the Beautiful are real began to collapse.
- The belief that Love is real began to collapse.

As Bertrand Russell is reported to have said, "I cannot see how to refute the arguments for the subjectivity of ethical values, but I find myself incapable of believing that all that is wrong with wanton cruelty is that I do not like it."

**What do you do if you grew up in a world in which value is not real?** A world without a source of value, without a Universe Story, without a story of human identity, without a story of desire, without a narrative of power?

**In the words of W.B. Yeats,** *the center does not hold.*

- You have a collapse at the very center of society, because you no longer have Eros.
- You no longer have a Reality in which value is real, and so you have this lingering sense of emptiness.
- You have a complete collapse at the very center.
- We become *the hollow men and the stuffed men*, gesture without form.

**And that's the source of our current existential risk.**

## THE DEEPER ROOT CAUSE OF THE META-CRISIS: A GLOBAL INTIMACY DISORDER

Above, I have outlined the major generator functions of existential risk. But there is a deeper cause for the existential risk that lurks underneath the rivalrous conflict governed by win/lose metrics and the fragile systems they engender.

And we cannot take the Death Star down without discerning and addressing this. We have already alluded to this root cause above, but at this point we need to make it more explicit so that, from this context, the adequate root response will become clear.

**Modernity threw out revelation, but was unable to establish a new basis for value.**

This ostensibly surprising statement can be understood in a few simple steps:

1. All of the catastrophic and existential risk challenges we face are global: from climate change to artificial intelligence, pandemics, systems collapse, and exponential arms races.
2. Every global challenge self-evidently requires a global solution.
3. Global solutions can only be implemented with global co-ordination.
4. Global co-ordination is impossible without global coherence.
5. Global coherence is only possible if there is a global resonance between the parts.
6. Global resonance is only possible if we have global intimacy.

## ONLY A SHARED STORY OF VALUE CAN GENERATE GLOBAL INTIMACY

Global intimacy—just like intimacy in a couple—is only possible when there is a shared story.

Not just a shared history, but a shared Story of Value.

- It is only a shared global story that can generate a new emergent quality of intimacy: global intimacy.
- A shared Story of Value must be rooted in shared ordinating values, or what we have called evolving First Values and First Principles.
- Intimacy requires a shared grammar of value as a matrix for a shared Story of Value.

**The global intimacy disorder is the root cause for existential risk.** The global intimacy disorder underlies the core generator functions for existential risk.

The global intimacy disorder is rooted in the failure to experience ourselves in a field of shared intrinsic value. This failure derives from the deconstruction of value.

Indeed, it is wholly accurate to say that **the root cause of the two generator functions of existential risk is the failed story of intrinsic value, or what we might also call the breakdown of Eros**.

1. The first generator function is **the success story**. Our modern success story is rivalrous conflict governed by win/lose metrics, which violates all the terms of the Intimacy Equation: there is no shared identity and no mutuality of recognition, feeling, value or purpose, and instead of *relative* otherness, there is *alienated* otherness. Such a story generates complicated fragile systems with no allurement or intimacy between the parts, systems which optimize for efficiency (as an expression of win/lose metrics) and not for resiliency and life.

2. The second generator function is **the deconstruction of intrinsic value** itself. The deconstruction of value is the sense that human value does not participate in the intrinsic value of the Real, for the Real is dogmatically declared to have no intrinsic value. Thus, there is no shared identity between the interior of the human being and Reality. There is no common participation in a field of shared intrinsic value. Instead of being intimate with value, we are alienated from value. And only intrinsic value can arouse will: political, moral, and social will.

To sum up, without a shared grammar of value there is no global intimacy, and therefore no global coherence, and no global coordination in response to catastrophic and existential risk, which means, put simply, there will be, quite literally, no future.

## HEALING THE GLOBAL INTIMACY DISORDER REQUIRES THE EVOLUTION OF INTIMACY

But we are not hopeless. On the contrary, we are filled with great hope. Hope is a memory of the future. That memory of the future *is* the direct hit that takes down the Death Star, the culture of death. **The direct hit must be**—as it has always been in history—**the emergence of a new stage of evolution.**

Crisis is an evolutionary driver, and every crisis is, at its core, a crisis of intimacy: from the oxygen crisis of the single cells dying which generated multicellular life at the dawn of existence, to the existential risk in this very moment.⁹

*The direct hit is therefore structurally self-evident: the evolution of intimacy itself.*

What is intimacy, as a structure of Cosmos all the way down and all the way up the evolutionary chain? We engage this inquiry in depth in other writings, but for now we will simply adduce what we have called the "Intimacy Equation":

> *Intimacy* = *shared identity in the context of [relative] otherness* × *mutuality of recognition* × *mutuality of pathos* × *mutuality of value* × *mutuality of purpose*

Intimacy is about the capacity of parts to generate a *shared identity* while retaining their otherness, or distinct identity. This requires multiple mutualities, including recognition, pathos (or feeling), value, and purpose. The parts must recognize and feel each other, even as they share value and purpose. But all of this must lead to intimate union—and not pathological

---

9   We demonstrate this principle in some depth in the multi-volume series, *The Universe: A Love Story* (forthcoming) (https://worldphilosophyandreligion.org/early-ontologies), *The Intimate Universe: Global Intimacy Disorder as Cause for Global Action Paralysis* (forthcoming), and in other writings of CosmoErotic Humanism.

fusion, where the distinct identity of the parts disappears—like subatomic particles that successfully become an atom, or two people who successfully become a couple.

## THE DECONSTRUCTION OF VALUE IS THE DECONSTRUCTION OF INTIMACY

We have identified the global intimacy disorder as the root cause of existential risk. But the underlying ultimate failure of intimacy is the deconstruction of value itself.

The deconstruction of value means that human value does not participate in any sense of intrinsic value of the Real. This is not about individual *values,* but about *the Field of Value* that underlies all of them. **When the human being**—moved, often sincerely or even nobly, by myriad cultural, historical, and psychological confusions—**claims to have stepped out of the Field of Value, then intimacy itself is deconstructed.**

The deconstruction of value is the deconstruction of intimacy.

In the absence of a shared Story of Value, a story that is an authentic expression of Reality's Eros, a story rooted in *pseudo-Eros* takes center stage and becomes the generator function for existential risk. Our modern pseudo-Eros story is *rivalrous conflict governed by win/lose metrics.* Such a story catalyzes in its wake the second generator function of existential risk: *complicated fragile systems with no allurement or intimacy between the parts.* It is in that sense that we have argued that the first generator function for existential risk is the success story.

- The failure of intimacy is precisely the impotent experience that there is no shared identity between the interior of the human being and Reality. **There is no shared identity in the sense of any kind of common participation in a field of shared intrinsic value.**
- **But only a shared Story of Value can arouse the global will**

**required to engage catastrophic and existential risk.** For it is only global political, moral, and social will—and we can even say *erotic* will—that can generate the most Good, True and Beautiful world that we have always known is possible.

## THE EVOLUTION OF LOVE IS THE TELLING OF A NEW STORY

Coupled with the Intimacy Equation is the scientifically grounded realization, in both the exterior and interior sciences, that Reality is a progressive deepening of intimacies, or, said slightly differently:

**Reality is Evolution. Evolution is the evolution of intimacy.**

- The evolution of intimacy requires—both personally and collectively—a deeper, more accurate discernment of the nature of our universe, ourselves, and our beloveds.
- This new discernment generates a new global Story of Value.
- The new global Story of Value generates an emergent, heretofore unseen global intimacy and heals the global intimacy disorder.

**The new Story of Value is the direct hit that takes down the Death Star and replaces it with the hope that invokes the memory of our best future.**

Global intimacy facilitates global coherence, which facilitates global coordination, which activates the possibility of our creative and effectively coordinated global responses to the global meta-crisis in its entirety and its specific expressions.

**To solve Bertrand Russell's challenge**—the apparent argument for the subjectivity of ethical values—**we have to reground value theory in eternal yet evolving First Principles and First Values, and articulate a new Story of Value.**

This is what we call CosmoErotic Humanism.

**CosmoErotic Humanism—together with other emergent strands—needs to become the ground of a world religion as a context for our diversity.** We need religion, even as we need science, to articulate a shared global grammar of value.

As we said at the beginning, our choice is simple: love or die.

- To love means to participate in the evolution of love, which is the evolution of the human Story of Value.
- To love means to evolve and activate a new cultural enlightenment—rooted in a new narrative of identity, a new narrative of value, a new narrative of intimate communion, a new narrative of desire, a new narrative of power—all of which will birth new narratives of economics and politics.
- The evolution of love is the telling of a new Story.

The new Story that must be told is a love story, for in fact that is the deepest truth of Reality, rooted in the best exterior and interior sciences, that we have at this moment in time:

- Reality is not merely a fact. Reality is a story.
- Reality is not an ordinary story. Reality is a love story.
- Reality is not an ordinary love story. Reality is an Outrageous Love Story.

Story doesn't mean it's *made-up*.

It means doing the hard work of integrating the validated insights of the traditional world, the modern world, and the postmodern world.

This is the intention at the heart of telling the new Story of CosmoErotic Humanism.

# ABOUT THIS VOLUME

In this critical time between worlds, technology is shaping the future of our lives, both as individual human beings and collectively as a species. Technology has brought great blessings in multiple vectors, and those benefits are regularly sung in the public sphere. But technology also threatens us with risks to our very existence on this planet. There are two forms of existential risk: the potential death of humanity—an extinction event—and the potential death of our humanity.

One primary cause for the death of our humanity is what we are referring to as the emergent "tech plex," an immersive digital temple disassociated from the Field of Value. At the heart of the tech plex is the "planetary stack" that currently wires the entire planet—the increasing interconnection of algorithmic and technological infrastructure, social structure, and superstructure that encircles the globe. The result is upgraded algorithms and downgraded humanity, which is one main cause for the potential death of our humanity, or what has also been called, by C.S. Lewis, "the abolition of man."

The notion that technology is value-neutral is simply not true. All technology is encoded with value—or tragically, with anti-value. For example, social media is encoded with the value of connectivity. But it is also coded with subtle but implicit anti-value: the deliberate intention to destroy our capacity for sustained attention outside of the tech plex. It intends to addict us, which it euphemistically calls "engagement." The catastrophic human consequences for mental health and human flourishing are incalculable. A second—and not at all unlikely—scenario is the emergence of artificial general intelligence (AGI), considered by many to be on the horizon, which is utterly alienated from the Field of Value.[1]

---

[1] See David J. Temple, *Invisible Architects: Skinner, Pentland & the Hidden Blueprints for TechnoFeudalism—Exit the Silicon Maze* (forthcoming).

## ABOUT THIS VOLUME

In order to avoid these forms of existential risk, we must respond with a new Story of Value. This story must be rooted in First Principles and First Values,[2] which are not mere social conventions that humans have invented but rather the inherent value structure of Cosmos that humans discover and evolve. All of Reality arises from the ground of what eastern wisdom called the Tao, the way, and which we refer to as the Field of Value. The Field of Value is the ground of eternal value that is ever-evolving. The tech plex, as currently conceived, experiences itself as disassociated from the Tao, from the Field of Value.

Although the tech plex is currently misaligned with the Tao, we can still discover that the Field of Value is both eternal and evolving. One expression of the Field of Value is what we have called "Outrageous Love." In the language of the new Story of Value, the only response to outrageous pain is Outrageous Love.

The set of "oral essays" featured in this volume, originally offered on the *One Mountain, Many Paths* weekly broadcast weave together the new Story of Value as articulated in CosmoErotic Humanism. The new story is a scientifically grounded, creative, and joyful response to the alienated tech plex that relocates us deep in the Field of Value that lies at the heart of the CosmoErotic Universe. We reconnect the immersive environment of technology with Evolution: The Love Story of Universe, whose plotline is the progressive deepening of intimacies, animated at all levels by the pulse of Outrageous Love.

*Volume 18*

*These oral essays are lightly edited talks delivered by Marc Gafni between October 2018 and March 2021.*

---

2   See David J. Temple, *First Principles and First Values: Forty-two Propositions on CosmoErotic Humanism* (2024).

# CHAPTER ONE

# SURVEILLANCE CAPITALISM: "WE'RE GOING TO STEAL YOUR EXPERIENCE WITHOUT YOUR PERMISSION"

*First Principles 02 — October 10, 2018*

### FIRST PRINCIPLES AND FIRST VALUES ACCOUNT FOR THE CRITIQUES OF NATURAL LAW AND PERENNIAL PHILOSOPHY

It is only by articulating a coherent and cogent vision of First Principles and First Values that we can navigate this eleventh hour of human existence, in which we stand poised between utopia and dystopia.

**By First Principles and First Values, we mean the very structures of Cosmos that evolve over time, but in their root they apply across all time, they apply across all space, and they live innately in every human being.**

Now, for those of you who are philosophers, I'm of course aware that there were two major attempts to articulate what I'm calling First Principles and First Values. One of them was the "natural law" school of thought, and the related but distinct attempt by what are called the perennial philosophers.

Both natural law and perennial philosophy have been in part correctly rejected by the postmodern academy.

*When we say First Principles and First Values, we mean something which is way beyond the early conception of natural law. It also takes into account all the critiques of natural law, responds to them, and evolves our conception of what natural law might mean. Our notion of First Principles and First Values also takes into account all the criticisms of perennial philosophy, and evolves our vision of what perennial philosophy might become.*

For those unfamiliar, perennial philosophy is a movement of early modernity that says that in premodernity, different religions and different systems were all arguing that they had the exclusive view of truth. However, **underneath all the surface structures of the different religions, there's a shared set of depth structures.**

This shared set of depth structures was extrapolated from all the different traditions, gathered and articulated by the early perennial philosophers.

**The problem with both perennial philosophy and natural law is that they claimed many things to be natural, depth structures of Cosmos.**

However, they were really surface structures, influenced by particular historical epochs, influenced by particular ways of thinking, or rooted in particular social moments—they actually weren't really depth structures.

That's a big idea.

## MISTAKEN ASSUMPTIONS OF NATURAL LAW AND PERENNIAL PHILOSOPHY

I'll just give you one example. There might have been, for example, a notion that particular kinds of sexuality are a violation of natural law, and that you should be burned at the stake, because "that's a violation of natural law." I'm giving an extreme example, but you get what I mean. That's actually not true, though. **That's not natural law. That particular vision of sexuality is actually a surface structure of Reality, not a depth structure.** That's an example of claiming something is a depth structure when it's really just a surface structure. That's an example of a mistake made in the name of natural law.

I'll give you an example from perennial philosophy. A classical mistake of the perennial philosophers is to say, "The only way to realize the full purpose of a human being is through a meditative path in which I nullify my sense of being distinct and I realize that I'm part of the great seamless coat of Cosmos, part of the Emptiness, part of the Field of One—I am True Self with all of Cosmos."

Now, that is true to some extent, but the perennial philosophers said that's the *only* way to come home, that's the only way to realize the purpose of human existence. So **they took one path and said that's the only path that can get you to the mountain—there is no other path**. As such, prayer was dismissed and it disappeared. Embodiment was really not part of the conversation at all.

There's a long list.

The emergence of the feminine, the balance between the feminine and the masculine, the evolutionary impulse, the notion that the human being participates in evolution, the balance between the dialectic between being and becoming—all of that was left out by perennial philosophy.

## CRITIQUES BY POSTMODERNITY OF NATURAL LAW AND PERENNIAL PHILOSOPHY

Postmodernity came to full fruition in the last thirty or forty years, but strains of it existed for the last 150 years. **Essentially, postmodernity critiqued and dismissed natural philosophy and perennial philosophy on multiple levels. These criticisms are true but partial.**

- Natural law made claims and said, "Oh, this is actually a depth structure," for example, a particular form of sexuality being forbidden, when that was really a surface structure. Based on those kinds of critiques, natural law was completely thrown out. It was basically said that natural law didn't take into account culture, that natural law fell into the "myth of the given," that natural law didn't understand all the influences that created our understandings of Reality—so natural law was dismissed.
- Perennial philosophy was thrown out for claiming one path as the only path, not realizing that it's many paths and one mountain.

Here's the key. **Postmodernism's favorite activity is to attack and kill perennial philosophy and to attack and kill natural law—because postmodernism has a hidden agenda.**

- Postmodernism says there is no shared narrative.
- Postmodernism says there are no universals.
- Postmodernism is a scathing attack on any form of universals and any form of a shared story of humanity.

And it has good reason for this, and bad reason.

The good reason is that postmodernism is traumatized by the premodern saying, *We've got the grand narrative and we're going to oppress everyone else who's not in our grand narrative.* Modernity had its own version of a grand narrative and anyone who is out of modernity's grand narrative gets oppressed. So postmodernity says, *No, these grand narratives are all wrong. Anyone trying to do a grand narrative is really hiding their drive for power. So we need to expose the true power motive and deconstruct all the grand narratives.*

**That's called the great deconstruction of postmodernity.**

## POSTMODERNITY'S CRITIQUE OF PERENNIALISM AND NATURAL LAW IS TRUE BUT PARTIAL, AND IT IGNORES RESPONSIBILITY TO ANY LARGER GRAND NARRATIVE—EXCEPT THE SUCCESS STORY

Foucault was an essential figure in this great deconstruction, but somewhere about halfway through his deconstruction he realized, *Wow, I'm deconstructing all grand narratives. I'm saying that there are no universals, there are no grand narratives.* Then he realizes, *But that itself is a universal. That itself is a grand narrative. I have a new grand narrative—there are no grand narratives. I have a new universal—there are no universals.*

*Foucault realized that was a performative contradiction: postmodernity was being radically arrogant and saying "there are no universals" but claiming that as a universal.*

In fact, that was the beginning of an opening of this very deep realization that natural law overreached and claimed surface structures as depth structures—for example, "this kind of sexuality is proscribed." I keep saying the example again so it's just very easy to follow.

It was also the realization that perennialism had overreached by saying, "This is the only path, the perennial philosophy," when actually there are many gorgeous and sacred paths that can bring you home and into the realization of our true nature and the true nature of Reality.

However, **both perennialism and natural law were doing something very important. This is what postmodernity ignores.**

There's a second reason for postmodernity's attack: it doesn't want to be responsible to any larger grand narrative.

- Postmodernity wants to be free.
- Postmodernity in this sense is a hyper-expression of modernity itself.
- Postmodernity wants to be free to be involved in this mad drive for material accumulation, for success.

The only narrative of the human being that does live in modernity/postmodernity is what we've called the "success story": a rivalrous story governed by win/lose metrics where the only goal is accumulation.

## THE NERVOUS SYSTEM OF THE PLANET IS THE WEB, THE WORLDWIDE VIRTUAL WORLD

Now, you might think that that's a little bit of an exaggeration. You might think I'm taking that too far. So I want to invite you to a particular book called *The Age of Surveillance Capitalism* by Shoshana Zuboff. It's actually a great work. It's not an easy read, but it's about the inner structure of the nervous system of the planet today.

> *The nervous system of the planet is the web, is the worldwide virtual world.*

Now, everyone who's listening now I assume has used Google, Facebook perhaps, Amazon, WhatsApp, and multiple other applications all over the web. These are all normal applications that we use. What we're unaware of is—as Zuboff points out very intensely, tracking original documents from the year 2000 until today—**what Google is really doing**. What happens is you do a Google search, but when you do a Google search what you search, how you searched, how you put in the query, all that information is captured.

In fact, what Google is doing is Google has created a crawling of the web over an unimaginable number of websites around the world. **Every time you put information into the web:**

- Let's say you use Gmail, **Google is reading your mail and drawing information from your mail.**
- How long did your mouse hover before you clicked on a link?
- How quickly did you make a decision?
- Every time you send a picture.
- Every time you send a text:
    ◊ How many question marks did you use?
    ◊ How did you use spacing?
    ◊ Did you make mistakes?

**What's actually happening is that your entire set of preferences**—implied from what you did, not what you said—**your personality, your emotions, everything you write… nothing disappears.** It's all being fed into an extremely complex artificial intelligence system driven by machine intelligence in order to build a profile of you.

Then you are able to be manipulated through predictive analysis in order to either sell you something or control you in a particular way.

## GOOGLE'S BUSINESS MODEL IS SURVEILLANCE CAPITALISM

For example, Google's business model is not about organizing the world's information, which is what Google began with. It was a public presentation. But in the early 2000s dot-com explosion, the bubble burst, and Google was pressured by venture capital funds that had invested in Silicon Valley. **Google then gradually shifted its operation and essentially became a** surveillance capitalist—a term coined by Zuboff—**which means *you're being surveilled all the time, for profit.***

Information about you is poured into a machine-intelligence-driven exponential AI supercomputer of the kind that's able to infer—from every jot and tittle that you write—your mood, your interior states, your preferences. An entire personality profile is then built around you and you start receiving highly targeted ads.

## FACEBOOK HIJACKS YOUR ATTENTION, TAKES YOUR INFORMATION AND TARGETS YOU WITH ADS, THEREBY COMPROMISING THE FREE MOVEMENT OF ECONOMY AND GOVERNANCE

Everything you put into Gmail or Facebook is read and registered. This is not Facebook "creating a platform to interconnect the world." That's not Facebook's business model. That's a lie. **Facebook's business model is taking all the information, all of your hijacked attention, downloading it into an artificial intelligence system, and then targeting you with ads.**

Those ads can be economic, but those ads can also be about health, and those ads can also be about how you vote.

All of democracy is built on the voter and the consumer. The free movement of economy and the free movement of governance is the innovation of democracy.

## WE ARE UNAWARE OF THE THREAT TO UNIVERSAL HUMAN RIGHTS

*Homo sapiens* first appeared about 100,000 years ago, and really only in the last several hundred years have we finally got to this huge innovation, this great evolution of consciousness—this great evolution of love called "universal human rights."

*Universal human rights means that your will is sacrosanct, that you have the ability to collate information and make free decisions, that you own your future, that your will has sacred integrity, that you're an irreducibly unique person with irreducibly unique value.*

These First Principles and First Values are completely ignored by Google, Facebook, WhatsApp, Verizon, Microsoft, Amazon. **The entire tech plex basically assumes that your experience, your interiority, your interior experience is raw material to be stolen and subject to analysis, out of which emerges highly predictive analysis, and then sold to advertisers**—corporations, political parties, etc.—**to manipulate you, move you to buy or vote in a particular direction.** However, you are unaware that all of that's happening. That's what's so unique.

Imagine that you're Kasparov playing chess in the famous Deep Blue match, and artificial intelligence wipes you out. But the artificial intelligence that beat Kasparov thirty years ago is now completely outdated. Google's AlphaZero recently played Stockfish, which represented that old artificial intelligence, and essentially decimated the old artificial intelligence. There's this new level of machine-learning-driven artificial intelligence that's exponentially more advanced than what beat the greatest reigning chess grandmaster thirty years ago.

But all of that is hidden from you, used against your ability to make a free decision.

- What happens to your integrity as a voter? It becomes a joke.
- What happens to your integrity as a consumer? It becomes a joke.

- What happens to a free economy and free markets? It becomes a joke.
- What happens to a free democracy? It becomes a joke.

## THE FAILURE TO ARTICULATE THE CASE AGAINST THE TECH PLEX IS ROOTED IN A FAILURE OF FIRST PRINCIPLES AND FIRST VALUES

Someone mentioned just now in the chat box, "this is in *The Social Dilemma*." *The Social Dilemma* is quite a good documentary, and the person who made it met with some people at the Center, one particular person, over the last year and had some great conversations. *The Social Dilemma* focuses on social media with a small conversation around the larger issues.

*The Social Dilemma* shares the same problem that Zuboff's book shares. The problem is that *The Social Dilemma* points out that **social media**—which is not exactly what I was focused on now—is **hijacking your attention**, and says correctly, "that's terrible."

But they're not sure why. They don't quite tell you why is it terrible that they're hijacking your attention? Aren't they just being like normal advertisers? *The Social Dilemma* movie can't quite answer that, so it says the reason it's terrible is *because it creates polarization: you get into a particular bubble of information and you keep seeing your own political views reinforced and exaggerated, so it creates great polarization.* **That is in part true, but that's not the core.**

---

> *Both The Social Dilemma and Zuboff's book miss the core of the whole thing. They're struggling to get it. They want to get it. They're on the edge but they can't quite articulate it.*

---

By the way, Shoshana Zuboff, the author of *Surveillance Capitalism*, appears in the documentary *The Social Dilemma* and she also struggles to articulate it. Tristan Harris, the gentleman who made *The Social Dilemma* with a bunch of other people, is struggling to articulate—they can't quite get there. **The reason they can't get there is because there's a fundamental failure of First Values and First Principles.**

Shoshana Zuboff is outraged that this is happening but can't quite understand why it's so wrong because she refuses to articulate any sense of an evolving perennialism—not the old perennialism but an *evolving* perennialism, an evolving natural law, or what we might call shared First Values and First Principles. She understands that there's this big violation here, but cannot say what it's in violation of. So you read the book and you get the outrage, you get what's happening, **but you're not quite sure why it matters.**

The same thing with *The Social Dilemma*, there's this outrage: *they're stealing my attention*. But big deal. Advertisers always steal our attention, that's what it's about. Why is that new? **Unfortunately, there's no understanding of First Principles and First Values.**

**First Principles and First Values means:**

- My interior experience is irreducibly unique.
- Feeling that experience is my source of wisdom.
- My attention and my unique quality of attention is my irreducible quality of the sacred.
- It's my attention that blooms Reality, it's my attention that's creative.

Under surveillance capitalism, under the tech plex, my ability to access my deepest quality of feeling Reality is blocked.

> *No one has a right to access my interior experience and then sell it to someone who's not me without my permission whose interests aren't aligned with mine.*

However, **you can't understand this violation without a deep articulation of Unique Self, which is one of the First Principles and First Values of Reality.**

Without First Principles and First Values, you can't move.

## SURVEILLANCE CAPITALISM: WE'RE GOING TO STEAL YOUR EXPERIENCE WITHOUT YOUR PERMISSION

I'm now going to read you six declarations of Google, which are now no longer published by Google, but were found by Zuboff in an early set of Google documents. Despite Google's current capturing of human experience, this was not their original intention. They created a search engine, and then they realized that **in the "exhaust" of the search engine, there was an enormous amount of surplus data.**

Then as the dot-com bubble burst they were attacked by their own entrepreneurs and funders, and they needed to figure out how to continue as a business. Since Sergey Brin and Larry Page were Stanford-educated postmodernists with no sense of First Principles and First Values, Brin says something like, "I didn't want to feel like a schmuck. I didn't want my Silicon Valley place to close." They were stuck in a success story governed by win/lose metrics.

Amit Patel was the particular person who really understood it, and he worked closely with Eric Schmidt a couple of years later. **They developed an entire model that**—because it was an unprecedented reality, and this computation structure had never existed before—**was not governed by law.**

*This is the Wild West*, as they would say in America. "No one's going to stop us because no one's thought of it. We're going to basically steal your personal experience without your permission." That's the core model of Facebook, Google, Intel, Oracle, Amazon, Microsoft, and all the rest.

In different ways, they're all doing the same thing. Their business model is surveillance capitalism.

## THE SIX DECLARATIONS OF GOOGLE

Here are the declarations. They're actually kind of shocking, and I'm quoting directly:

> 1. "We claim human experience as raw material for the taking. On the basis of this claim, we can ignore considerations of individuals' rights, interests, awareness, or comprehension."

Do you get the insanity of that? For example, **you sign a waiver whenever you get a new app. It says "agree" or "disagree," and there's this long contract that would take you two hours to read that no one ever reads, which bypasses genuine consent, in which you agree to unbelievable things.**

---

*You're agreeing to have all your data stolen and sold to third parties, but you don't even know what you're reading.*

---

The average person takes fourteen seconds, according to one study, to read those contracts, which aren't really contracts. They're "un-contracts," as Zuboff calls them. **They're violations of the notion of contract.**

So back to the declarations:

# THE EXISTENTIAL RISK OF TECHNOLOGY

1. "We claim human experience as raw material for the taking. On the basis of this claim, we can ignore considerations of individuals' rights, interests, awareness or comprehension."

2. "On the basis of our claim, we assert the right to take an individual's experience for translation into behavioral data."

Meaning: everything you did—every hovering of a mouse, every exclamation point, every question mark—is all fed into this AI monstrosity, which then uses machine learning to translate your experience into a new shadow script.

- It's a shadow script that's only readable by the new technological priesthood.
- This new text is readable only through this machine intelligence that then conducts auctions—millions or billions per second—**selling your information in order to target you for some version of manipulation unbeknownst to you, and that violates your will**.

3. "A right to take, based on our claim of free raw material, confers the right to own the behavioral data derived from human experience."

4. "A right to take and to own confer rights to know what the data discloses."

It's beyond shocking.

- "We have a right to take your experience."
- "We have a right to turn it into data."
- "We have a right to own your data."
- "We have a right to know what the data discloses."

So the personality profile generated by machine intelligence—the engine of artificial intelligence, which you're unaware is happening, that then builds a profile to manipulate you—we own that. *We have a right to know all of this about you even though you didn't give us permission.* **Why? Just because. We're just claiming it.** It's a completely made-up claim. And **the only way you can make up a claim like this with such vicious audacity is if you have no First Principles and you have no First Values.**

## INSTEAD OF SOLVING EXISTENTIAL AND CATASTROPHIC RISK, OUR BEST MINDS ARE CAUGHT IN THE SUCCESS STORY

If there are no First Principles and First Values, then:

- There is no irreducible Unique Self.
- There is no *Homo amor*.
- There is no Love as a First Principle.
- There is no interior quality that needs to be honored and supported.

"I'm not responsible for the emergence of a Unique Self Symphony. None of that's true. None of that exists. That's just a social construction of reality after all," say Larry Page, Sergey Brin, Mark Zuckerberg, and a host of others, along with tens of thousands of the best data scientists who've been absorbed into the tech plex drain. It's a tragedy.

> *We need our best minds and our best scientists to solve existential risk and catastrophic risks. We need our best interior scientists, who are articulating First Values and First Principles, working with our best exterior scientists, who can develop external solutions. Exterior and interior need to move together.*

## THE EXISTENTIAL RISK OF TECHNOLOGY

But what's happening today is that the best scientists are being absorbed into the tech plex because they're being paid enormous salaries. Each one of these scientists and their families are caught in a rivalrous success story governed by win/lose metrics. **So we're actually draining the best minds in the world in order to develop the best way to get more and more surplus behavioral data—these are behavioral futures about you that are sold against your interest.**

All of this is happening all the time. And you think that you're being benefited with "these really sweet apps," that "Google and Facebook are really lovely because they gave you a free email account," that "they're free," and "they give you a sense of empowerment." So basically, **the world of the web is playing to your need for empowerment** and may serve you in all sorts of ways.

It's not that Facebook doesn't do many good things or that Google doesn't do many good things—of course they do. But those good things are a mask for this deeper dystopia.

## FROM HOLDABLES TO WEARABLES TO BIOMETRIC SENSORS

Imagine when we go from holdables—you hold your phone, you hold your computer, you're downloading data—to wearables—which is Bluetooth or Google Glasses and all sorts of devices and clothing being made today in what's called the Internet of Things.

*We're developing more and more what's called the Internet of Things, which means that all of the world will become a virtual web.*

Why do you think there's Google Earth? Why do you think there's Google FaceTime view. **These are all taking pictures of all domains of experience**

**and feeding it into the Google plex, the Facebook plex, the Oracle plex, the Microsoft plex monster.** That's actually what's happening.

Now imagine the third level: biometric sensors, under-the-skin sensors—we're very close to that. The reason people are going to use them is because they can predict cancer in thirty years. See, all these things have good uses. Your health can be better served by biometric sensors, which are already beginning to be used around the world, meaning *an under-the-skin chip in order to give you the best health in the world—and also for you to be part of the grid, because if you're not part of the grid you don't exist: you won't be able to get a job or get insurance.*

So by that point you've got holdables (your phone, your computer), wearables (Bluetooth, your Google Glasses) and all sorts of other structures that are going to become part of what's called the Internet of Things. It's the clothing of your life, whether it's a thermostat in your house or whether it's in your bed—smartphone, smart thermostat, smart bed.

And then come the digital assistants. **It's a move to appeal to people to empower them.** *We're going to give you what the rich people have. The rich people have digital assistants. Now you're going to have a digital assistant.*

Isn't that great? **But your digital assistant, just like your smart thermostat and smart bed, are gathering data about everything that's happening and feeding that data into the system.**

Now, maybe you say that *there's a place where you can say no and not agree to share your data*. However, if you read the contract carefully it says that if you don't agree to share the data then most of the good features that make the system run well are not guaranteed or will be disabled. There's a little blackmail in the system. People spend fourteen seconds reading the contract, and *if you read the contract and say no, what you've bought actually won't work*. Wow!

Here are the last two Google declarations.

5. "A right to take, to own, and to know confer the right to decide how we use the knowledge."
6. "A right to take, to own, to know, and to decide confer our right to the conditions that preserve our rights to take, to own, to know, and decide."

Which means *it's our decision how to use the knowledge, and it's our right to do everything we can to fight any law or any change in the status quo that would challenge our right to own your interior experience.* Does everyone get this?

**The only reason this is possible**—and this is what *The Social Dilemma* and Shoshana Zuboff's *Surveillance Capitalism* missed, though they are both great works—**is because as a society:**

- We are without a sense of Unique Self.
- We are without a sense of the value of interiority.
- We are without a sense of the unique value of your unique interior experience.
- We are without a sense of First Values and Principles of Cosmos.

## FIRST PRINCIPLES AND FIRST VALUES REFUTE SURVEILLANCE CAPITALISM

With First Principles and First Values, we know that:

1. Cosmos is evolution.
2. Evolution is growth and transformation.
3. The purpose of my life is to go through a unique trajectory of my own unique growth and transformation.
4. I need to place my attention on my interiority in order to facilitate my own deepest growth and transformation. This is my greatest joy, allowing me to give my Unique Gift and live my unique life.

Those are all First Values and First Principles. They're not dogma. We've spent the last ten years at the Center for Integral Wisdom working on articulating the best vision of these First Values and First Principles, and we're going to spend the next five or six years writing them into a Great Library. It has to be as perfect as it can be. But without these First Principles and First Values, Shoshana Zuboff's rage is sputtering, which means she can't quite express it—and I'm reading her intensely, because she's necessary reading. She cites the poet W.H. Auden in order to express her rage, but that doesn't take you home. Every time she tries to express *what values are they violating*, she comes up with some general, insipid, broad sentences that fall way short of true First Principles and First Values.

**She's outraged, but since she's essentially a postmodernist**—at least that's how she presents publicly—**she has no way to articulate her rage.**

I don't know Tristan Harris, but he's worked with some people at the center, with one of my colleagues. He's certainly a lovely young man, and he did a great job in *The Social Dilemma*, as did the people who worked with him. **But he has no articulate sense of the First Values and First Principles that are being violated.**

Your attention and the unique quality of your attention are part of the irreducible structure of your Unique Self.

> *Your Unique Self is not your separate self. It's not a social construction of Reality, and it's not your Myers-Briggs test. Your Unique Self is an irreducibly unique quality of desire and intimacy.*

Unless you validate uniqueness as a First Principle of Cosmos and validate the evolution of uniqueness as Unique Self—**without that depth of knowing there is no way you can object to the tech plex**. So that's the tragedy of Shoshana Zuboff: she falls short, she sputters. *The Social Dilemma* also sputters in the end—and that's what it was critiqued for.

It's going in the right direction but is not based in First Principles and First Values.

It's a big deal.

## EXPOSING THE INNER STRUCTURE IN WHICH HUMAN EXPERIENCE IS BEING STOLEN

What I've tried to do is, number one, **to expose, to make clear, to make visible the inner structure in which human experience is stolen by the tech plex.** Colonized is too nice of a word. It's outright robbery, which is what a lot of colonization was, but I want to just call it robbery.

- It's an original sin.
- It's outright violation.
- It's a fundamental rape of an individual's interiority, but it's rape even without their knowledge.

**And it's selling that interiority in a way that's misaligned with that person's essential interest.**

Now, it's taken me the last decade to be able to articulate this clearly, and we're going to spend the next years writing about this. We're writing an entire volume on this particular dimension.

I hope for a lot of people, once you hear this, it's like, *Wow, I kind of knew that all along.*

That's the nature of a great insight. Now it's obvious. It's beautiful in that it's so obvious.

**That's what we've called for the last five years: the reconstructive project.**

> *The reconstructive project is to reconstruct First Principles and First Values that will help us understand the violation, and so we can then be activated against the violation.*

## ACTIVATION: THE DIRECT, FIRST-PERSON EXPERIENCE OF REALITY COMING ALIVE IN ME

Here's the last point. I want to just play off the word "activated." You have to have a first-person experience of your value. You have to be activated. **One of the First Principles and First Values of Cosmos is what we want to call activation.**

- You can call it transformation.
- In some of the mystical traditions, they called it "ascension."
- In other traditions, they called it the "great descent."
- But really what it means is that **you access directly an experience of Reality, and experience of Infinite Value lived as you.**

**You transcend the limited identity of ego**—you don't leave ego behind, you don't leave your separate self behind—**you evolve beyond exclusive identification with ego, and you come alive to your own inner nature.**

- You watch Beethoven's *Ode to Joy* being played in a public square in Italy, and you're filled with this larger sense of yourself.
- You do profound meditation.
- You do ecstatic prayer.
- You dance.
- You do a practice of writing Outrageous Love Letters, but

# THE EXISTENTIAL RISK OF TECHNOLOGY

not as a mere writing practice—you're writing so that you actually *become* Outrageous Love.
- You realize that you're lived as love.
- You realize that you're lived as joy.
- You realize that Infinity manifested you—finitude—as a unique expression of Infinite Value itself.
- You realize that you're infinitely needed and infinitely desired, infinitely honored, infinitely intended by Cosmos, that you're both held by Infinity and that you participate in Infinity itself.

You must have a direct first-person experience. You can't have someone tell you that it's true unless they're telling you in a method that we call transmission. My hope is that you can hear in my voice the truth of this.

You don't have to work out the conceptual structure, just recognize, *oh, you can feel the truth of that*—that's the truth of Reality coming alive in you. It's non-conceptual.

**It's the infinite value of you**—not because you're a commodity and not because you're being sold to advertisers for personalized ads or to manipulate your vote. No!

- You're irreducibly gorgeous. Your unique quality of intimacy, unique quality of presence, unique quality of joy, and unique story are celebrated and needed by all of Cosmos. And you disclose to Infinity a face of Herself. Wow!
- Your story needs to be fully lived and fully told and your gift fully given—because that's what it means to be alive in this world.

**The direct experience of that is what—with total trembling humility—I'd love for you to feel in this moment.**

Can you feel that? Let the ego go. Just scream *Yes. Yes!* My integrity is in that *Yes*. Our integrity lives in that *Yes*, friends. That's where our integrity lives. Wow!

We can't just paint an intellectual picture. We can't just engage in practice.

**We have to be fully activated, fully alive. We have to become not** *Homo sapiens*. **We have to engage the transformation, the apotheosis in which we literally participate in that Infinite Value.**

In the last several years, in the last several weeks particularly, I've read maybe a thousand intense documents from different court cases, early Google documents, Facebook documents—and the intensity of this is beyond imagination.

*We have to actually expose and deconstruct and obstruct and stop this moment in history. We have to reshape it.*

The argument against stopping it is that *it's inevitable*—but it's not inevitable. **It's only inevitable if there is no larger story.**

It's inevitable if Sergey Brin and Mark Zuckerberg and Larry Page are driven by a success story governed by win/lose metrics. It's inevitable if the exponential profits of a very narrow sector, one percent of the population, drive reality. **But it's not inevitable in any other way.**

- It's time for a revolution.
- It's time to stand.
- It's time to articulate policies and articulate a new direction.

**Over the next year we're going to be thinking about what the policies should be, but one of the possibilities**—and it's not yet formulated—**is for people just to get off social media en masse.** Wow! It's not yet an easy possibility. Social media has a lot of good to it.

So how do we change social media? How do we change Facebook? How do we change Google?

The first activism, where it has to all begin, is in articulating First Values and First Principles, by coming together and letting go of own egoic ambition and stepping into a Unique Self Symphony. We then become a cascading force of Spirit, of revolutionary joy, of audacity that becomes a revolution that changes the course of history. That's what we have to do now.

**We have to inhibit "inevitability" and articulate First Values and First Principles which are the basis for the great revolution.**

Wow! Thank you for being with us.

Thank you, everyone.

# CHAPTER TWO

# DIAGNOSING THE TECH PLEX: FROM DIGITAL DICTATORSHIP TO DIGITAL INTIMACY, FROM SOCIAL SELF TO UNIQUE SELF, FROM SOCIAL HIVE TO UNIQUE SELF SYMPHONIES

*First Principles 09 — January 31, 2021*

## EVOLUTIONARY LOVE CODE: THE UNIQUE SELF IS UNDER ATTACK BY THE TECH PLEX

The Unique Self is the inward space of uniquely lived experience in which meaning is discovered.

The Unique Self is under attack in multiple ways, including the assumption of Big Tech and Big Data that the human being is no more than a social self, the assumption of the spiritual traditions that the human being is either a True Self or an Obedient Self, and the shared assumption of the entire rest of the world that the human being is a separate self.

The cultivation of Unique Self consciousness is the overriding moral imperative of this moment in history.

## THE ARTICULATION OF UNIQUE SELF CONSCIOUSNESS IS THE OVERRIDING MORAL IMPERATIVE OF THIS GENERATION

I want to spend a couple of minutes on Unique Self consciousness. For now, I just want to state or say it, and then widen the lens and see **the three primary ways that Unique Self is challenged**, and **why the Unique Self is the single most important idea in the world today to alleviate suffering**; to bring hearts together, to move beyond polarity, and to respond to the existential risk, which is quite literally the death of our humanity—because we actually cease to be human beings in the deeper sense of what a human being means—and the physical death of humanity itself.

## SEPARATE SELF, SOCIAL SELF, TRUE SELF AND UNIQUE SELF

What is Unique Self?

- Unique Self says that the human being is not merely a separate self. I'm not just a skin-encapsulated ego.
- I'm also not merely a social self. I'm not merely in a web of social relationships.
- I'm also not merely True Self: One with Consciousness beyond my personal story. My true essence is not only an impersonal participatory part of the One.

Each of those has relevance, and each of those is important.

I'm not just separate self, but there is a dimension of a human being that's separate; separation lives in the mind of God. That's my sense of being individuated. There's some truth to that, but it's partial; I'm much more than a separate self. I actually don't exist independently of the All. I'm a unique emergent of the All. I don't exist independently of everything. I am nothing without everything. I'm dependent on it all, and it all lives in me, as me, and through me.

At the same time, I'm not just a social self. I'm not just a node in a network that's affected by all of the prior causes. I'm more than that.

I'm also more than pure consciousness. I'm not just awareness or awareness of awareness, as the Enlightenment traditions try to tell us. Yes, I am awareness underneath my body, underneath my emotions, and underneath my thoughts. There's still an eye, and a dimension of that eye is awareness. So I'm not just my thoughts, I'm not just my emotions, and I'm not just my body. I am—that's True Self—but I'm not just that.

---

*I'm not just a separate self, I'm not just a social self, and I'm not just a True Self; I'm a Unique Self.*

---

## UNIQUE SELF: I AM IRREDUCIBLY VALUABLE AS A UNIQUE EMERGENT OF THE WHOLE

Unique Self says that on the one hand, I have a dignified separate self story that's absolutely true, but that separate self story is not all I am.

I'm also one with the Field of Consciousness, but not just the Field of Consciousness. I'm one with the Field of Consciousness, Desire, Eros, and Intimacy. The Field of Consciousness is alive. It's teeming with Eros, intimacy, and desire. But I'm not just one with that Field, I'm a *unique expression* of that Field; I'm a unique emergent, unlike any other.

I'm both part of a social web, and I'm a separate node in that social web. But I'm not just separate—I'm one with the web; the entire web in some sense lives in me, and all of consciousness lives in me.

- I'm affected by the whole thing,
- I'm a unique emergence of the whole thing,
- I am irreducibly valuable as a unique emergent of the whole thing.

That's the quality of person that's Unique Self.

## YOUR UNIQUE SELF IS YOUR UNIQUE RESPONSE-ABILITY TO REALITY

My uniqueness lives in an evolutionary context. **I'm a unique expression of the evolutionary impulse itself that beats in me, and my deepest heart's desire is the desire of evolution itself.**

That's Unique Self, and it's the answer to the question, *Who are you?*

I'm going to state the Unique Self formula, and with that context, we're going to dive into our topic. If you're new and you've never heard the Unique Self context, this is a very short statement of it. If you've been with us for a decade, it's getting newer and newer all the time. **It doesn't get older; it develops every single time we express it, every single time we experience the realization again.**

Unique Self is the answer to the question of *who are you?*

> *You are an irreducibly unique expression, or emergent, of the LoveIntelligence and LoveBeauty that is the initiating and animating Eros of All-That-Is; that lives in you, as you, and through you; that never was, is, or will be ever again, other than through you; and as such, you have unique capacities; and you have unique capacity to give your Unique Gift and live your unique story that's needed by all that is; to give your Unique Gift that's needed in your unique circle of intimacy and influence, to live the unique pleasures of your life;* ***and to fulfill your unique responsibility, your unique ability to respond to Reality.***

That's very deep.

**Your Unique Self is not just Reality acting on you.** That's the social self. The social self says, "Reality acts entirely on you." There's a great sentence in *Walden Two*, B.F. Skinner's utopian novel about what society should be, and in many ways the basis for the worldwide web. We'll get to that in a couple of seconds, but I'll just give you one sentence. Frazier, the lead character in *Walden Two*, says: *You have to set up certain behavioral processes which will lead the individual to design his own good conduct. We call that sort of thing "self-control." But don't be misled, control always rests in the last analysis in the hands of society.*

Meaning: "You actually don't act upon the world. You think you do, but you don't. The world acts upon you." Unique Self says *No!* to that.

- Unique Self says that you have a unique response-ability.
- Your Unique Self is your unique response to Reality.
- And that response is generated internally.

**Because the Field of Consciousness and Desire lives uniquely in you—** and therefore, you're not merely responding to the cues that you've received through various forms of nudges and social pressures—**you're actually acting on Reality from within**. The world may appear to act on you, but you actually act on the world.

---

*Your unique response to Reality—that's your Unique Self. That has irreducibly unique value: your response to the world, your gift to the world, and your unique way of living and being.*

---

## YOUR UNIQUE SELF HAS IRREDUCIBLE VALUE AND IS YOUR CURRENCY OF CONNECTION

Even if you don't have a job in thirty years because machine intelligence has obsoleted most of the jobs:

- You have a Unique Self.
- You have a Unique Gift.

- You have a unique way of living, laughing, loving, and being.
- There's a poem only you can write.
- There's a song only you can sing.
- You have a unique set of insights.
- You have a unique quality of intimacy.
- You have a unique configuration of desire that's you.

**That's the essence of Unique Self: irreducible value.**

Through mastering the instrument of your Unique Self, you actually don't alienate yourself, because Unique Self is not separateness. You realize that **uniqueness is not the structure of alienation; uniqueness is the currency of connection.**

*Uniqueness joins you with, and uniqueness makes you a part of. Your Unique Self instrument allows you to play your instrument in the Unique Self Symphony.*

So now we have a narrative of intimate communion. That's our context. That's Unique Self.

### B.F. SKINNER: THE HUMAN BEING IS A SOCIAL SELF

Now I want to try and go deep with you, because we have to diagnose correctly what's actually happening.

By the way, somebody mentioned Brené Brown. She is doing a decent job, and I think she's making a great contribution in terms of healing shame. However, she stops talking about shame at a surface level of separate self. She does a good job at the psychology of separate self, but doesn't access the qualities of the True Self, Unique Self, or the evolutionary context:

Evolutionary Unique Self or Unique Self Symphony. So she's doing a very good job at organizing separate self, at level one. But it's a great level and she's doing a great job at level one. So more power to you, sister!

Now I want to try and share with you something so dramatic, so shocking, and so disturbing. We're going to respond to it—the revolution has to respond to it.

**It's a moral imperative to transform this dimension of Reality.**

There was a very well-known behavioral psychologist named B.F. Skinner, who was at Harvard for several decades. Skinner talks about a set of ideas which were profoundly attacked and condemned in very fundamental ways. Chomsky wrote a very famous essay reviling Skinner. The reason is because **in the way Skinner was understanding Reality, he understood the human being as being primarily what I'm calling**—echoing Skinner—**a social self.**

> *Skinner basically says the human being is only a social self.*

He talks about this in a book called *Beyond Freedom and Dignity* and in *Walden Two*, his utopian novel published after World War II. Skinner is actually coming from a very important place; he's misread and misunderstood.

**He's absolutely wrong because the human being is much more than a social self, but where he's coming from is very important.**

## B.F. SKINNER: LET'S NULLIFY THE AUTONOMOUS MAN, THE INNER MAN

I want to read you a passage from Skinner, from *Beyond Freedom and Dignity*. Skinner says:

> We need to abolish the autonomous man—the inner man, the possessing demon, the man defended by the literatures of freedom and dignity—his abolition has long been overdue. He has been constructed from our ignorance, and as our understanding increases, the very stuff of which he is composed vanishes, and it must do so to prevent the abolition of the human species. To man qua man—this autonomous man, this inner man—we say good riddance. Only by dispossessing him can we turn from the inferred to the observed, from the miraculous to the natural, from the inaccessible to the manipulable.

This is an incredible paragraph.

For example, Shoshana Zuboff, in *Surveillance Capitalism*, quotes this paragraph in horror, but her horror is both correct and incorrect. She doesn't fully understand Skinner's motivation and where he's coming from. So what does Skinner say in this paragraph?

**What Skinner basically says is that we need a technology of social behavior.**

But why does Skinner say it? Chomsky attacks him, and Zuboff is aghast; correctly so. Skinner is basically saying *let's nullify the autonomous man and let's nullify the inner man.*

## SKINNER'S APPROACH—NULLIFYING THE AUTONOMOUS MAN—IS THE BASIS OF SOCIAL MEDIA

Now we're going to show that Skinner is the basis of social media—the basis of Facebook, the basis of Google—and that **there's a direct line between behaviorism and Skinner, surveillance capitalism and the tech plex.** Once we realize that, we understand what's animating the web, and therefore understand how we have to respond: to deconstruct the web as it exists now and create an entirely new vision of what the web needs to look like.

We need to create a Facebook, but it has to be a Unique Self Facebook.

We're going to draw a direct line from Skinner to Facebook, and we're also going to take issue with the people who critique Skinner, like Shoshana Zuboff, without actually understanding his motivation. **Her failure to understand his motivation and provide an alternative enormously weakens her critique of the web** in *Surveillance Capitalism*—and makes it actually ineffective in the end. Just like the important movie *The Social Dilemma*, *Surveillance Capitalism* doesn't actually understand the web, or the underlying structure and motivations of the people who were trying to animate it that way. So they simply reviled and dismissed them.

**Shoshana Zuboff reviled Skinner. She realizes his relationship to the worldwide web, but doesn't understand its motivation. We've got to go much deeper.**

Let's go super deep. We're literally breaking new ground in culture now, and we have to madly step in. So here we go.

First, Skinner is a utopian—we've got to get that straight. He realizes that we need to recast society. Because in the 1950s, 1960s and the 1970s, and even as early as before World War II, Skinner realizes that we're facing existential risk; he is one of the first to really get existential risk. This is something that Zuboff completely misses. In the passage which I just read, what does he say? He's talking about creating a technology of behavior *in order to prevent the abolition of the human species.*

---

*What is the abolition of the human species? That's existential risk. That's what he's talking about.*

---

In his introduction to *Walden Two*, his utopian novel, he places himself in the lineage of those who tried to offer new narratives of human identity. So he talks about Buddha, and he talks about Thoreau. In other words, **Skinner, in *Walden Two*, is trying to reformulate human identity.**

Why? Although Skinner places himself in the general lineage of new formulators of narratives of identity, he doesn't directly use Buddha's work in any direct way—but Skinner gets Buddha's critique of the separate self. **Skinner's books** *Beyond Freedom and Dignity* **and** *Walden Two* **are based on the threat of existential risk and the realization that existential risk is going to come from a separate self gone berserk.** This is exactly what the Buddha was afraid of.

Buddha says, "The thinking that I'm only a separate self is an illusion, but that illusion creates *dukkha*, or suffering." So Skinner says, *Yes, in Buddha's time, that illusion created suffering. But in our time*—as he watches the emergence of nuclear power, as he now adds to that exponential technology, which creates exponential risk—*the separate self doesn't just create dukkha, but the separate self is going to destroy reality. Actually, together with exponential technology and nuclear power, the separate self will be the abolition of human society entirely.*

That's what Skinner is talking about.

> *Skinner realizes the threat of existential risk pretty much before everyone else did, and he's saying that the way to respond to existential risk is to formulate a new vision of the human being.*

## C.S. LEWIS VS. SKINNER: THE ABOLITION OF MAN, THE ABOLITION OF HUMAN SOCIETY

There's a book from 1943 called *The Abolition of Man*, written by C.S. Lewis. He says that the abolition of man is going to come because in forty, fifty, or sixty years—he doesn't give an exact date—**there's going to be an omnicompetent state which develops irresistible scientific**

**technologies. That omnicompetent state is going to label themselves as the "conditioners," and they're going to attempt to socially condition human beings in order to have an engineered safe society.** Then he says, that's going to cause the abolition of man.

But by the abolition of man, C.S. Lewis means not existential risk in the sense of the death of humanity—through exponential technology, nuclear proliferation, or climate change. He's talking about the existential risk which I've been referring to which is not the death of humanity, but the death of *our humanity*.

When Lewis talks about the abolition of man, he says that **it's going to be brought about by the conditioners, those people, in his language, who have stepped out of the Tao. By stepping out of the Tao, he means they've stepped out of the experience of living within intrinsic value structures.** They've stepped into a kind of reductive scientific materialism, which says there is no intrinsic interior value in Cosmos. C.S. Lewis talks about the Tao, this intrinsic interior value, as this form of universal natural law.

He says that if we step out of the Tao, out of this natural law which binds all human beings, what's going to happen is, in a few generations, there's going to be new technologies and the conditioners are going to appear. And these conditioners are going to initially intend this for the good of Reality.

That's what he says on page twenty-four, paragraph five:

> They'll initially intend the good of reality, but in the end, because they've stepped out of value—they've stepped out of the Tao, because in the end they're materialists—it's going to be the power of the few over the power of the many. They become despotic, and it's going to actually destroy human beings.

**People who will be controlled and conditioned will no longer be human beings as we currently experience.**

Now, when C.S. Lewis talks about the abolition of man, he says, it's going to happen through the "conditioners" developing technologies of human behavior. Who's he referring to? He's referring to Skinner, but no one notices; no one even reads the book anymore. It's an unbelievably important book, written in 1943, in the middle of World War II, as we realized the emergence of human power, and **we realized we don't have a story equal to our power**.

When C.S. Lewis talks about the conditioners who are going to cause the abolition of man, he's talking about Skinner, who views the human being as being a social self and as being *manipulable*, which is exactly the word Skinner uses. Lewis says, *Wow, that's the most dangerous thing in the world*. Although Skinner hadn't yet published *Beyond Freedom and Dignity*—he published that book in 1971— Skinner's basic ideas of behaviorism and the conditioners were already available; they were already in the *zeitgeist*, so Lewis was already aware of them in a meta-sense.

**C.S. Lewis views the danger as being the conditioners—i.e. the behaviorists—who are formed by a kind of reductive, pseudo-materialist neo-Darwinism; a scientistic rejection of interiors; not scientific, but scientistic and dogmatic, fundamentalist rejection of interiors; a stepping out of the Tao or stepping out of value.**

He says, *this is going to cause what we're calling an existential risk to our humanity*; he calls that the abolition of man, and he faults Skinner.

Thirty years later, Skinner then says to C.S. Lewis, *you got it wrong*, and he uses the words "the abolition of human society." Of course, what he's saying is that *those people who insist on the individual, the dignity of the separate self*, which is of course the Christianity tradition and the Platonic tradition, and the Greek tradition. In other words, this is the Western tradition of the dignity and freedom of the separate self, which Skinner is ascribing to C.S. Lewis, the tradition that affirms the value of the separate-self human being—and *which is going to cause the abolition of human society*.

Notice that he uses the same phrase. So there's this hidden conversation between these two great thinkers. C.S. Lewis is saying, without mentioning Skinner, "You're going to cause the abolition of man; the death of our humanity." Then, Skinner says back to C.S. Lewis, "You just don't get it, my friend. We're facing existential risk to the very existence of humanity, and that existential risk comes from the separate self."

## HOWEVER MISGUIDED, SKINNER IS RESPONDING TO EXISTENTIAL RISK AND CRITIQUING SEPARATE SELF AS THE SOURCE OF HUMAN DIGNITY

Now the Western idea is that human dignity and freedom is rooted in the separate self, and this is what Shoshana Zuboff gets so excited about. She says, "How could Skinner reject the dignity of the separate self? That's crazy, you can't do that." Then he embraces the social self, which Zuboff views as a disaster. **She's right, it is a disaster to embrace the social self exclusively as your model of self.** But she doesn't get what's happening.

> *Zuboff doesn't get that Skinner is responding to something important; he's responding to existential risk.*

Skinner is not a crazy man of Harvard, he has actually adopted and up-leveled Buddhist critique of the separate self. So he's saying, Buddhist critique of the separate self is real. Zuboff, who gets that Skinner is kind of an antecedent to the web, is all aghast. She's like, *how could Skinner reject the separate self?* Because **Zuboff is standing in the tradition of Western Enlightenment, which has the separate self as the source of all dignity**; this is Chapter Five of the *Unique Self* book.

But Skinner, although he's not quoting Buddha directly, he's phenomenologically embracing that critique of the separate self. He's saying the separate self is not the source of human dignity. That's why Skinner calls his book provocatively *Beyond Freedom and Dignity*. What does he mean?

**What Skinner means is we've got to move beyond the Western notion of separate self, which if you put it together with exponential technology, it's going to destroy us. Because separate self causes *dukkha* (suffering), but separate self with exponential technology destroys everything.**

That is, separate self with exponential technology is what we've called before "rivalrous conflict governed by win/lose metrics," which is the modern success story. **That false narrative is one key generator function of existential risk.** The person who gets that is not Zuboff, writing *Surveillance Capitalism*, but Skinner who she's critiquing; he totally gets that.

**What Skinner says is that *we need a different model of self*.**

## SKINNER DID NOT HAVE THE TOOLS TO DEVELOP TECHNOLOGIES OF HUMAN BEHAVIOR

In 1990, Skinner died frustrated because, he says, *We don't have the machines and methods to generate a technology of human behavior, and so we're going to wind up with the abolition of human society*—again, playing off of and critiquing C.S. Lewis, without mentioning him by name. He's says, *Your notion of the human being as a separate self who lives within these value structures is all very nice, C.S. Lewis, but that's a premodern idea, and a bad idea. It's an idea that the religions have made central, but it's actually wrong; we have got to get rid of separate self.*

**Skinner dies before he's able to accomplish any of this**. Lamenting, he says, *I wish I had what the physicists had*. The physicists have real mathematical equations. They can manipulate objects, and they enabled all modern science.

All the progress of modern science is based on mathematical measurements done by physicists. Skinner says, *Tragically, we don't yet have mathematical models that allow us to develop technologies of human behavior, which can map the human being and relationships between human beings. So, therefore, I can't get anywhere with this.*

## ALEX PENTLAND, ONE OF THE ARCHITECTS OF THE WEB, IS A DIRECT CONTINUATION OF SKINNER

**After Skinner died, along comes an entire new generation of data scientists.** One classic representative is Alex Pentland, who wrote a book called *Social Physics*. Pentland shared this with our friend Howard Bloom, who's a senior scholar at the think tank and a great thinker. Pentland said, "I'm one of the major architects of the web" in a personal conversation a bunch of years ago, when Howard's book, *The Lucifer Principle*, came out. Pentland is right—he is one of the architects of the web.

In *Social Physics*, Pentland never once mentions Skinner because that's political suicide, but **what he says is a direct continuation of Skinner.** He's actually the completion of Skinner, if you will, in the following way. Pentland says, *We now do have the machines and methods to do this. We have data science, and data science is a new mathematics. With this new mathematics, we can track the human being, and the human being is not a separate self.*

That's what Pentland states in an essay he wrote, called "The Myth of Individuality."

*Pentland agrees with Skinner that we need to facilitate the death of the contemporary Western notion of individuality.*

He has gaggles of doctoral students who've each started their own companies, and those companies are embedded in relationships with Google, Facebook, and the entire tech plex. They're based on the notion of a social self, but this social self now can be manipulated. These are Skinner's words: "We need to move from the inaccessible to the manipulable," but not because he wants humans to be manipulated in a bad way.

Skinner is a utopian, but he's a utopian without First Values and First Principles, and that's why he's dangerous.

- Skinner is a utopian, he gets existential risk. So he's correct in saying that C.S. Lewis was too caught up in the separate self of Western society.
- But where C.S. Lewis was right is that he knew *we have to live within the Tao, within frameworks of value*, whereas the materialist Skinner has stepped out of frameworks of value.

He's influenced by existentialism, logical positivism, and neo-Darwinism. He developed behaviorism, which basically considers the human being as an "It": a social self that you can influence through social nudges, social cues, social pressure, through a technology of human behavior that's mathematically developed through data science.

Skinner's vision in *Walden Two* is of a socially engineered society, which he wants not because he's a terrible guy. He's not a Stalinist totalitarian, but rather a *technocratic* totalitarian, if you will. But he's not a totalitarian in the sense that he wants to rip your soul out—not at all.

Skinner is afraid of the separate self, so he wants to organize human society in a way that's safe. He understands the risks, but he's a utopian who has stepped out of the Tao.

- That's where C.S. Lewis was right in *The Abolition of Man* when he talks about the conditioners who've stepped out of the Tao. He's referring to Skinner, and he was absolutely right.
- Skinner was also right in responding to C.S. Lewis, saying, *If you just stay with the separate self, you're going to get to the abolition of human society,* playing on C.S. Lewis's phrase "the abolition of man."

## PENTLAND: DATA SCIENCE IS THE NEW PHYSICS WHICH WILL ALLOW US TO ENACT A NEW VISION OF SOCIETY

We now need to go the next step. So you've got Skinner in *Beyond Freedom and Dignity*, his major book from 1971. What does he mean when he says beyond freedom and dignity? He means that *the old notions of freedom and dignity based on the separate self will bring about existential risk, the destruction and the abolition of humanity.*

> *Skinner says, we've got to move to a new self, the social self. After Skinner dies, Alex Pentland says, without naming Skinner, that we didn't have the physics to do this, but now we have social physics.*

He calls his book *Social Physics*, and he talks about *data science as the mathematical structure that's going to give us this new physics that's going to allow us to enact this new vision of society.*

## THE FOUNDERS OF THE TECH PLEX ADOPT THE VISION OF SKINNER AND PENTLAND

Now, who are the people that Pentland and Skinner have influenced? Who has adopted their vision? The answer, **quite literally, is the founders of the tech plex**.

Let's take Mark Zuckerberg, who says, "Our goal is creating a global community." Larry Page says, "Our goal is a societal goal. Our goal is not incremental change, but revolutionary change."

If you read the inner text in some of the public texts of the founders of the tech plex, they adopt Skinner and Pentland's utopianism. Pentland is directly and personally involved, through many doctoral students who have formed companies and partnerships throughout the tech plex.

## SOCIAL MEDIA IS AN EXPRESSION OF SKINNER'S WALDEN TWO

Now here's where it gets a bit creepy. But we have to get the diagnosis in order to change it. So when you look at let's say Facebook and Google's mottos, they seem very benign and lovely:

- "We connect people everywhere."
- "We organize the world's information."
- "We bring people closer so that they can express themselves."

What is this? These are actually expressions of Skinner's *Walden Two*, expressions of the social self. **Notice that the entire tech plex**—all of the social media platforms, Facebook, Google, the whole story—**is built around social nudges, social cues, social pressure: likes, how many views you get, sharing personal information, etc**. So what happens? Here's the mechanism: You share your data, and Google collects your data.

It doesn't ask you for it; it decided that it has a right to it. Google has six declarations.

1. We have a right to take your data without asking you or without any real informed consent on your part.
2. We have a right to feed that data into machine intelligence.
3. We're going to get out of machine intelligence a personality profile about you, about "your inner demons;" about what moves you and drives you.
4. We own that secret text about who you are.
5. We have a right to sell that text to third parties because we own it.
6. It's sold to third parties who are misaligned with your values. It's sold by automatic machine-intelligence-driven auctions.

Now, **what would give Google**—and Facebook and Microsoft and Samsung and Amazon, the list goes on—**the right to think that they can take your data, which is the fruit of your personal experience**? Only what C.S. Lewis described as **a stepping out of the Tao, as a stepping out of First Values and First Principles.** Because once you step out of the Tao, then you're no longer governed; you become the conditioners that C.S. Lewis describes.

C.S. Lewis described these conditioners as having this benign smiling face, who say they're doing sweet and nice things for you, and they give you all these trinkets and free apps—Gmail and WhatsApp—and they're organizing the world's information, connecting people everywhere, and "bringing the world closer together."

But what they're actually doing is fulfilling Skinner's vision of *Walden Two* and Pentland's vision of *Social Physics*, which is based on stepping out of the Tao, out of the Field of Value.

## WE NEED TO REPLACE THE UNDERSTANDING OF NATURAL LAW WITH EVOLVING PERENNIALISM, AN EVOLVING SET OF FIRST VALUES AND FIRST PRINCIPLES

Now, C.S. Lewis got the Tao partially wrong. He actually identified the Tao, or value, with natural law, which is a weak idea; natural law is not sufficient. There are a lot of weaknesses in natural law—for example, it doesn't get evolution. We have to critique natural law.

---

*We've replaced natural law with what we're calling Evolving First Values and First Principles, which is a shared narrative of human universals that are evolving.*

---

That's really important. In that sense, it's why people like Zuboff are so afraid to embrace First Values and First Principles, because they identify them with C.S. Lewis's natural law. This is where his Christianity got him in trouble; he was too influenced by Aquinas's view of natural law, which is a mistake. Natural law is not just eternal and unchanging.

In fact, **we need to replace natural law with an evolving perennialism, an evolving set of First Values and First Principles**. That's one of the core pieces of work at the Center, to understand that there's an evolving set of First Values and First Principles. That's really important.

Let's get back to our major thread. So C.S. Lewis predicts that the conditioners will step out of the Tao, that they'll step out of First Values and First Principles. So we're going to then have a set of utopian thinkers, like Skinner and Pentland, who don't have First Values and First Principles.

What's the model of utopian thinking sans First Values and First Principles? Mao, Stalin, Lenin.

Communism is precisely a utopian move, which disqualifies the Universe by saying: *There are no First Values and First Principles.*

## THE TECH PLEX: WE ARE ORGANIZING SOCIETY AS SOCIAL SELVES

So now what do you have? You've got Zuckerberg, Page, Brin; the entire tech plex, and its view of itself is that their *organizing society*—they talk about it all the time:

- "We are the change engine of society."
- "We, at this time of a threat, are going to create global community."

It looks very sweet, but it's not sweet; it's creepy. Meaning, there's a direct line between Skinner and Pentland and data science, which says that the human being is a social self—therefore, to borrow Skinner's phrase, the *human being is manipulable.*

Now, that's precisely half right. The human being is a social self that you can manipulate through social nudges and social cues. But that's precisely only one quarter of the human being, because **a human being is not just a social self.**

> *Skinner's critique of separate self is correct, but his conclusion is wrong.*

Skinner and Pentland's reductive materialist conclusion is that the human being is not a separate self at all, but a social self. But that ignores an enormous amount of validated conclusion and insight, both from the exterior and interior sciences. The human being is only partially a social self.

The human being is not only a social self, but is also a True Self. **The human being is also irreducibly valuable because the human being is inseparable from the entire Field of Consciousness and Desire.** Every human being participates in the one True Self, and the total number of True Selves in the world is one. Every enlightenment science and every interior science in the world has a notion, based on direct experimentation, of a deeper self than separate self and social self. We call that True Self.

## TRUE SELF AND UNIQUE SELF ARE IGNORED BY THE TECH PLEX

True Self is ignored by Skinner, ignored by Pentland, and ignored by the tech plex. Not only is it ignored, but **the tech plex is built on attention-hijacking. When your attention is hijacked, you don't have the ability to access the inward space of meaning and practice.** There's no possibility of focusing inwardly to realize through genuine practice your true identity, which is, *I'm not merely a skin-encapsulated ego, I'm not merely the illusion* *of separate self.* Skinner is right about that, but that doesn't mean I'm only a social self; I'm also True Self. I am consciousness itself.

But I'm not only True Self, I'm actually Unique Self.

*Each one of us who is True Self sees through a unique set of eyes.*

I have:

- A unique perspective
- A unique quality of intimacy
- A unique configuration of Eros and desire
- A Unique Gift to give
- A unique poem to write
- A unique song to sing

*I am an irreducibly unique expression of the LoveIntelligence and LoveBeauty that is the initiating and animating Eros of All-That-Is.*

So therefore, the goal is not the social hive or the superorganism of social selves that Pentland and Skinner talk about. The goal is not the social hive that's manipulated by social cues, or what Pentland calls *the nervous system of the planet*, which Pentland identifies with the web.

That's not what we're going for. That's not the strange attractor of society.

## UNSEEN, PENTLAND AND SKINNER HAVE FORMED THE THINKING OF THE TECH PLEX, WHICH ARROGATES TO ITSELF THE RIGHT TO YOUR EXPERIENCE

Pentland and Skinner have secretly—meaning they're not actually hiding it, but they're also not openly declaring it—formed the thinking of the tech plex and of the entire enterprise of surveillance capitalism, **which arrogates**

**to itself the right to your experience**—because they've stepped out of First Values and First Principles. That's what C.S. Lewis was referring to when he predicted it seventy years ago. He said, "The conditioners are going to step out of the Tao, and once they step out of the Tao, then they're going to become the man-molders." He's referring to Skinner's vision.

## PERSONAL DATA IS CURRENTLY BEING USED BY MACHINE INTELLIGENCE ALGORITHMS TO COMPROMISE THE TWO BASIC IDENTITIES OF DEMOCRACY: THE VOTER AND THE CONSUMER

After Skinner dies, Pentland, along with many other data scientists, develops the mathematical models, and then says, *Hey Facebook, Hey Google, let me collect everybody's data, feed it into machine intelligence, and develop personality profiles.*

Then, based on that precise information, we'll be able to directly influence the outcome of an election, for example, because we're going to know every wavering voter, and we're going to know the unique social pressure points to exert on this group of voters to make them vote in a particular way.

We're going to know exactly how to make people buy exactly what we want them to buy. **We're going to upend the two basic human identities of democracy, which are the voter and the consumer.** Democracy is going to become a sham because there's no real voting, because all of the machine intelligence is arrayed against you to manipulate your voting choice—and you don't even know it's happening.

Machine intelligence is not minor, we're talking about technology that's so sophisticated that it's completely defeated the old machine intelligence that defeated the best chess matchers in the world in the 1990s. **An exponentially more powerful machine intelligence is arrayed against you to exert a form of behavioral engineering to impact your decision-making, both as a consumer and a voter.** This is now being deployed in democracies, and it's just the beginning.

## UNDER-THE-SKIN SURVEILLANCE IS THE NEXT STEP AND WILL RESULT IN DIGITAL DICTATORSHIPS

As we move from over-the-skin surveillance to under-the-skin surveillance—deploying biometric sensors, which everyone is going to need in order to join a health system, to get insurance, or to get a job—**there's going to be so much data coming in that those who own the data will essentially create digital dictatorships.**

- There might be a veneer of democracy, but democratic elections are going to become a joke.
- There might be the veneer of an economy, but your independent decisions as a consumer are going to become a joke.

The entire drama of human decision-making is going to be upended.

## THE POSTMODERN DECONSTRUCTION OF VALUE TOGETHER WITH SURVEILLANCE CAPITALISM RESULTS IN THE "CONDITIONERS" PREDICTED BY C.S. LEWIS

Now here's the paradox. In Big Tech, you have this utopianism that they've adopted from Skinner and Pentland. But because the Big Tech founders are all postmodern—meaning, value has been deconstructed—there's no belief in actual value. As Yuval Harari says in several of his books, *it's all fiction and social constructions of reality; there is no genuine Unique Self, no genuine True Self, and no irreducible human value; value is a complete human fiction.*

**When you marry the postmodern worldview with surveillance capitalists of the tech plex, you get the "conditioners" who've stepped out of First Values and First Principles, creating this behavioral engineering system. Predicted by C.S. Lewis, that's the scenario that we're in now.**

> *The response to this is to develop and share a new model of self and a new Universe Story.*

People like Zuboff must get it. She doesn't quite get it yet. She justly critiques Skinner but doesn't understand that he's responding to existential risk.

People like Pentland and his data scientists must get this new model of self and a new universe story as well. **The new model of self is True Self and primarily Unique Self and Evolutionary Unique Self; the move from *Homo sapiens* to *Homo amor*.** But at the core of everything is the Unique Self model.

We have to infuse the tech plex—the data algorithms of the nervous system of the planet—with Unique Self. Unique Self has to be the animating energy of the nervous system of the planet.

## WE NEED TO RESPOND TO SOCIAL SELF WITH UNIQUE SELF

We need to respond to social self with Unique Self. We need to respond to reductive materialism with the Universe: A Love Story, the Amorous Cosmos. These new narratives and this evolution of the source code is essential.

That evolution of the source code needs to then infuse the source code of the data algorithms that are now hijacking authority in society today. Authority in society today is moving from governments to algorithms—but algorithms are written by human beings, and human beings are being downloaded into algorithms. **But the value that's been downloaded into algorithms is the social self, the postmodern or "social construction" values of Skinner and Pentland, all the way through the tech plex.** So when we read Google and Facebook's lovely slogans, we realize, *Oh my God, this is Skinner in disguise.*

> *The response is the radical downloading of Evolutionary Love, of Homo amor, of Unique Self, of the Amorous Cosmos, of the Intimate Universe, into the tech plex. This takes us from digital dictatorship to digital intimacy.*

The digital world is not the enemy. The hijacking of attention for the sake of social control is the enemy.

## THE POWER AND PROFIT AGENDA TOGETHER WITH UTOPIANISM, SANS FIRST PRINCIPLES AND FIRST VALUES

Now in this last piece, let's notice one more insidious dimension of the tech plex that we can't miss: **These surveillance capitalists have married the direct profit and power motive.** Meaning Sergey Brin, Larry Page, and the whole gang, have tens and tens of billions of dollars of individual net worth, because **they've profited from harvesting your data in violation of the First Principles and First Values of personhood.**

> *There's this immense greed motive, there's this immense power and profit motive, and they've married with utopianism in the tech plex without First Values and First Principles.*

Surveillance capitalism is absorbing all of your personal experience as data bits, pouring them into machine intelligence, then constructing your personal personality profile—using data science, mathematical algorithms, and machine intelligence—which includes your points of social pressure and manipulation. And then they sell it.

- The more data they get, the more accurate predictive analysis becomes, and the more profit it generates for Facebook.
- Facebook and Google this quarter did better than they've ever done before, despite all sorts of public attacks, because they're getting more and better data and therefore selling more and better predictive analysis to third parties.
- The greater your data set is, and the more developed your machine intelligence is, the more you're able to develop predictive analysis.

## IMAGINE WHAT HAPPENS WHEN A DICTATORSHIP OWNS DATA

Imagine what happens when a dictatorship owns data. Forms of this are now being used by China. *This is actually happening now.*

- Think about the social control there.
- Think about how sophisticated artificial intelligence has become.

**Therefore, we need to convene the world around a shared new story based on shared First Values and First Principles.**

One of the first questions we need to address when we create global intimacy is: *Who owns the data?* The data can't be owned by private companies in this particular way because *whoever owns the data runs the world.*

> *If the data is owned by a bunch of private companies, which are owned by about twenty-five people, we have the "conditioners" who are able to run the world despotically.*

## IN THE ABSENCE OF UNIQUE SELF, SOCIAL SELF BECAME THE ANIMATING ENERGY OF THE NERVOUS SYSTEM OF THE PLANET

What we've done here is diagnosis: **We've identified the mixture of surveillance capitalism with its profit and power agenda, together with utopianism—Skinner and Pentland responding to existential risk. That utopianism being adopted by the founders of the major players in the tech plex, who are all surveillance capitalists. And all of them are postmodern, that is to say without First Values and First Principles.**

Although he died before postmodernism really took hold, Skinner was actually an early postmodernist. Skinner was a behaviorist and a materialist, who basically said, *interiority is off the table*. He was not a bad guy, and he was a beautiful utopian. *Walden Two* is a beautiful book. Skinner himself stood for value, but he just thought that value was socially constructed, because with his view of universal values, he said, *there's no way to articulate that*. He rejected C.S. Lewis's natural law. And he was partly right in rejecting it; Lewis's natural law actually didn't understand evolution.

I'm sure that Skinner would have loved our notion of evolving First Principles and First Values, and I'm sure he would have come on board in that, and I think he could have come on board with a notion of True Self and Unique Self. But those models didn't exist in society during his time. The only model that existed was separate self.

So, Skinner says, *We have to move beyond the freedom and dignity of the separate self*—not because he was a bad guy, like Zuboff says—but because he didn't have a sense of Unique Self, so he could only go to social self. **So partly through his influence, the social self became the animating energy of the nervous system of the planet.**

## OUR JOB IS TO ENGAGE IN A RECONSTRUCTIVE PROJECT OF VALUE SO WE CAN MUSTER THE NECESSARY OUTRAGE AGAINST THE TECH PLEX

So what's our job? We're going to evolve the source code of culture and consciousness, and evolving the source code of culture and consciousness is the evolution of love. What we've tried to do here is crack open what's going on all the way on the inside; what's animating the tech plex.

Here's the paradox: **Shoshana Zuboff gets exactly half of it.**

In other words, she's horrified at the tech plex. She does a magisterial job of detailing sixteen different structures of surveillance capitalism. But she doesn't understand the following critical points:

1. She pretty much ignores the objective existential risk that we're facing, and only mentions it a couple of times.
2. She herself has stepped out of the Field of Value. So she gets really angry at the tech plex, but she can't root her anger at the tech plex in First Values and First Principles because she's speaking a kind of postmodern story, rooted in modernity, which says that value, including the value of the individual, is at best a social construction—but it's not more than that.

Paradoxically, Zuboff says that *it's really important to name surveillance capitalism because only if we name it can we actually transform it*—but she won't name First Principles and First Values.

So, she says, *I'm going to arouse astonishment and outrage when people realize what surveillance capitalism is doing.* **But you can only be genuinely outraged when you experience that there's an *actual* violation of value—objective value, real value, not socially constructed value.**

---

*If value is just fiction, then maybe the social self is the best way to go. It's only when you get the First Value and First Principle of personhood and uniqueness that you're truly outraged.*

---

**The reason Zuboff doesn't adopt First Values and First Principles is because she doesn't have a conception of it.** She thinks all there is natural law, which was dismissed by the Academy, so *the best we have is the old liberal order.* But here's the deal, postmodernity took down the old liberal order. Throughout her book, she refers to the liberal values of individuality, but postmodernity took those down entirely; that's all been thoroughly deconstructed. So we have to now engage in a reconstructive project.

**It's only in a post-postmodern reconstructive project, in which there's a set of evolving First Values and First Principles, that we can actually muster the outrage that Zuboff magisterially and gorgeously seeks to invoke.**

But without First Values and First Principles, we don't know why we should be outraged that Google has decided that it owns our data. It's not against the law. It was unprecedented in 2000 when Google decided to mine the data exhaust of our web participation and then realized that that data exhaust would be converted by machine intelligence into a text and sold to third parties. **It wasn't against the law. It wasn't against anything except for First Values and First Principles.** But no one had articulated First Values and First Principles, because postmodernity said *it's all a social construction of reality.*

So paradoxically, Zuboff herself is, in some subtle sense, allied and aligned with the overlords of the tech plex, whom she attacks—because both of them refuse to embrace First Values and First Principles.

**Zuboff relies on the old liberal order, which is easily explainable as a social construction and as a fiction, while the postmodernists of the tech plex adopt the social self because they don't have any First Principles and First Values, such as uniqueness or personhood.**

We're not here to get angry at anyone. We're not here to be outraged at this reality. These are not bad people—these are great people.

But *it's our job to actually make the da Vinci move*. We're at a time between worlds, and we're at a time between stories.

**The overwhelming moral imperative for those with eyes to see is to take our seat at the table of history and evolve the source code.**

For this we need:

- A new narrative of identity
- A new narrative of self
- A new universe story
- A new narrative of communion: not a social hive but a Unique Self Symphony
- Not social self but Unique Self
- Not natural law but evolving First Values and First Principles

# CHAPTER THREE

# THE NEW EXISTENTIAL RISK: NOT THE DEATH OF HUMANITY BUT THE DEATH OF OUR HUMANITY—THE DEHUMANIZING CREEP OF MACHINE INTELLIGENCE

*Episode 222 — January 10, 2021*

## WE'RE HERE TO TELL THE NEW STORY

What a moment this is. What an incredible moment. We literally stand poised between utopia and dystopia.

The utopia is more beautiful than we can possibly imagine. It's our obligation, our responsibility, and our delight to imagine it. Oh my God.

The dystopia—the unimaginable level of pain and suffering, the loss of all the Good, the True, and the Beautiful—also lurks at the door.

Often, we're caught up with false flags. We're caught up in what seem to be dramatic events, but that's not where the action is actually happening. The action is happening someplace else, quietly. There are creeping annexations of our very personhood, **creeping transformations of what it means, at the very core, to be a human being.** We barely notice they're happening until they're upon us, and we're trapped on the inside. Oh my God.

The most potent response we have is to feel the evolutionary impulse moving through us, to speak as the leading edge of evolution and tell a new story—not a fanciful story, not a conjecture, not a made-up story, but the best integration we have in the world today.

> *We bring it all together—the hottest, most beautiful, and most true integration that we have in the world today of the deepest structural interior and exterior insights of all of the great traditions of premodernity, all of the great understanding and insights and sciences of modernity, and all of the wisdom of the best parts of postmodernity—and weave it together in a seamless embrace of a new story.*

That new story is what we are here to tell.

I'm spending an enormous amount of time, friends, reading the literature, and trying to comb Reality to understand where we are. Let me just ask you a simple question: *If your cell phone were taken away and all of your devices were taken away for twenty-four hours, what would you do? How would you feel?*

Most people in the world who are connected through their devices would feel terrible, devastated. Virtually all people below the age of thirty-five would feel nauseous and sick, and virtually all people below the age of twenty would border on breakdown and intense nervousness and anxiety.

Let me ask you some questions:
- Why would that be true?
- Where did your inner self go?

# THE EXISTENTIAL RISK OF TECHNOLOGY

- Where was our attention stolen away to?
- Who is it? Who is the "we"?
- What is the force in the world that entered into your interior and recast your own inner experience without your permission?

It's so powerful that the overwhelming majority of people below thirty-five today would fall into some state of depression if they were disconnected from Instagram, Facebook, Twitter, social media, etc.

That's shocking. And it's so much deeper than that.

To really get what's going on and where the genuine threat to society is—**to understand it as a new form of existential risk**—I want to invite you to step into this.

## EXISTENTIAL RISK: THE END OF HUMANITY

Let's set our intention. There are two forms of existential risk. We've never quite framed it this way, but it's really elegant and critical to understand.

**One form of existential risk comes from objective factors**, which are either various forms of disaster or interior social dynamics that work in a particular way. A disaster might be based on political structures that we haven't deconstructed: for example, a nuclear device goes off. That's a shocking issue that needs an enormous amount of conversation.

> *We think that the threat of a nuclear explosion has gone. It's not. It's just gone from the headlines.*

I've done an enormous amount of study on this issue in the last four months, as one form of existential risk.

## EXISTENTIAL RISK DUE TO RIVALROUS CONFLICT

Then there's another structure within this first form, which has to do with what we've called the "rivalrous conflict" that defines Reality.

> *We live in a story of rivalrous conflict.*

Rivalrous conflict is governed by win/lose metrics that drive the extraction model in which we take critical resources from the Earth that it took billions of years to create. But it also drives exponential growth curves, which always fall off, and **it creates a vast, fragile system, which by its very nature is self-terminating.** That's a second structure within this first form of existential risk.

Climate change and nuclear weapons are forms of existential risk that are all part of the first structure. These are different subsets in the first form. Let me make it more specific.

The notion of artificial intelligence run amok, which Nick Bostrom at Oxford's Future of Humanity Institute has written so much about in the last twenty years, is a form of existential risk where AI follows its own interior imperative and basically takes over the story. That's not impossible. There's a significant chance of this happening if we don't monitor how AI develops in the next seventy, eighty, ninety years.

Those are all things we need to look at very, very carefully.


## WE NEED A NEW STORY OF VALUE GROUNDED IN FIRST PRINCIPLES AND FIRST VALUES

We have to change our essential story of humanity. **It's only by changing the story that we change the interior source code of Reality and begin** to develop the common will—the shared global coherence—to address existential risk.

It's only by telling a new story that we understand that we are actually part of a shared humanity. This new story is based on a universal grammar of value, a shared set of First Principles and First Values that we all agree to, and that are already available to us.

It's never been done before.

---

*We need to articulate these First Principles and First Values in order to get to a universal grammar of value, which will then displace the win/lose metrics of rivalrous conflict, which is the generator function for this first set of existential risks.*

---

Part of our intention here is to tell this new story of Reality, which is this Evolutionary Story, this Love Story. It's not a casual love story, not an ordinary love story, but a full understanding of Reality as Eros: Eros animating the four fundamental forces, Eros expressed as intimacy, Eros being the evolution of intimacy.

Holding that set of considerations, and with your permission, I want to move to a different form of existential risk. The first form of existential risk to humanity is that we're going to somehow wipe ourselves out based on any of the scenarios, which I briefly alluded to now.

Humanity will disappear because systems will collapse as a function of any of the reasons I've mentioned up to now, plus a few others. That's one form of existential risk to humanity.

I spent all this time creating this context because context here is everything.

## THE ARTICULATION OF A SECOND FORM OF EXISTENTIAL RISK: THE DEATH OF OUR HUMANITY

We are a band of revolutionaries committed to evolving the source code of consciousness and culture, which is the source code of love. We're committed to a Planetary Awakening in Love through Unique Self Symphonies. We're trying to create a shared field of understanding that we can all step into together.

Then, **we become activists in the field of Reality.**

We begin to move together as this small group of people, just a few hundred of us at the core, and then a few thousand at the second core, and others listening from around the world. As Margaret Mead said, *it's only a small group of people, radically committed to each other*—evolutionary family—*who can change the world.*

I want you to get the context for this new way of looking at this, this new way of saying it.

---

*The second form of existential risk is the creeping annexation of our humanity.*

---

**The second form of existential risk to humanity is** not that humanity is destroyed by one of these factors that I've described but **that we'll stop being human.** The existential risk to humanity is *that, in some fundamental way, we'll stop being human or that what it means to be a human being won't be available to most people.*

That's an entirely new form of existential risk. It's not existential risk to humanity because something's going to happen to us; it's rather what I would call **an annexation of humanity creep.** It's a gradual "creep" in that it's slowly, incrementally embracing us and at some point, **we literally stop being human as we understand it.**

## THE EXISTENTIAL RISK OF TECHNOLOGY

All of the things that define human beings actually disappear:

- You're thirty-five years old; you can't disconnect from your iPhone.
- You've got all these ads coming at you all the time, competing for your attention.
- You're completely sucked into how many likes you got, and how much approval you got, and how many thumbs up, and how many thumbs down, and you feel nervous and filled with anxiety disconnecting from your device.

That's the beginning of your *dehumanization*.

---

*You're no longer just a human being; you and your device are actually one.*

---

**Then we shift from *holdables*—devices that you hold—to *wearables*.** We wear either a biometric sensor on the outside or a biometric sensor on the inside, and everything is tracked. *Wow!* These biometric sensors then combine with your smartphone, your smart thermostat, and your smart bed. It's called "the Internet of Things," *IoT*, or sometimes it's called, "ubiquitous computing," where the goal is seamless connection with your devices.

One of the ways the Internet of Things is infiltrating society is through the rise of *digital assistants*. Alexa is a digital assistant that people are increasingly using all over the world.

All of these devices are recording data all of the time:

- Your digital assistant
- Your biometric sensor
- Your smartphone
- Your smart bed
- Your smart appliances

## THE DEHUMANIZING CREEP OF MACHINE INTELLIGENCE

- Your WhatsApp or any of the "free" apps that you use all the time.

**They record everything you do.**

All this data is then sent to a central, organized system, which is driven by and animated by machine intelligence, which then analyses not just what you did or said or which websites you visited…

*Machine intelligence is able to analyze your mood, how you feel, what your likes are, what your dislikes are, what your preferences are.*

It begins to know you in ways better than you actually know yourself, and it's then able to *manipulate* your actions in many ways.

There's a current sense of *ever-encroaching machine intelligence, which is getting more and more pervasive*. We're just at the beginning of it.

- We're just at the beginning of biometric sensors.
- We're at the beginning of the Internet of Things.
- We're at the beginning of the attention economy that steals your attention.

All of this data is recorded and then fed into this machine intelligence processes, which is using advanced machine intelligence of the kind that is exponentially more powerful than the early machine intelligence used to defeat chess champion Garry Kasparov. All of that develops a personality profile on you, and then begins to monitor you more closely, and then it begins to nudge you this way and then to nudge you that way, and then to invite you here and to invite you there.

Then, it begins to offer voting suggestions.

We're at the very beginning of a process where the human being as we know it is beginning to disappear. **We're living in a worldwide technocracy mediated by the web, in which "anomalies"—meaning people acting out of turn with "acceptable behavior"—are monitored, and then rewarded or punished.**

- There's no in-person person to speak to anymore.
- Everything is determined by the system driven by Big Tech, which we might call "Big Brother" or "Big Other."
- Big Tech is acquiring and absorbing your information by giving you all these free little apps, then creating a personality profile, then nudging your action.
- This undermines any sense of free will and individual personhood, and creates a hive intelligence, a hive of humanity, a machine hive.

*Just like the factory in the twentieth century determined social relations, now the machine intelligence hive is going to become the dominant modality. The human being as we know it will disappear.*

Now, if you think I just made that up, you should read the writings of a certain MIT professor named Alex Pentland, one of the most prestigious scholars in the world today with gaggles of doctoral students and lots of influence in the tech world. He is the successor to B.F. Skinner, the behaviorist who was one of the key articulators of everything that's driving the web today.

Pentland writes in one major paper, called "The Death of Individuality," that this is good news because, for him, the individual is a separate self and, *There is no real separate self; we're really just "social" selves, and so we need to come together in this organized hive intelligence to eliminate suffering and address the growing threats in the world.*

Pentland and dozens of people around him in that small group of influential technology priests are driving the development of machine intelligence, which drives Google and drives the whole story. It drives Facebook and Microsoft, and everything you're interacting with.

He's talking about moving beyond free choice, moving beyond individuality—he thinks individuality is a joke—and he's being cheered on all over the world. In addition, that group of data scientists is working closely with governments: both with Western democracies and places like China.

Friends, you want to know what the threat is? Watch out for false flags. When everyone puts their attention on a false flag, that's an indication that the true threat is being obfuscated.

*This second form of existential risk is that we cease to view the human being as human—because we don't have a story of what it means to be a human being. A human being becomes a "cog"—a computational, digital object, to borrow the exact phrase spoken by the CEO of Microsoft—to be moved and manipulated for the greater social good.*

We're already so close to it; it's actually beginning to happen. The fragrances of it are everywhere and no one's noticing.

This form of existential risk to humanity is *the death of our essential humanity*. **Our essential humanity depends on us having a self-understanding.** And we gain this by answering the following questions:

- Who am I?
- Who are we together?
- What's the relationship of the I to the we?

Within culture today, there are literally no good answers to these questions. No one's even talking about it. **We're lost in this old, outmoded sense of being merely a separate self, "social" selves, or sometimes in the enlightenment sense, the true but partial belief that "we're all part of the same One."**

But actually, Alex Pentland and all of the students at MIT:

- Those who have started dozens of companies that are driving and animating culture.
- Those who are the key guest speakers in culture, and the best-selling authors.
- Those people who are writing all the papers that are animating and defining Google and Facebook and the entire social media world.

None of them have ever heard of Unique Self. They've never heard of what we call a Unique Self Symphony. For them, Eros is not even on the table.

What's happened?

1. Fundamentalist religion has been dismissed because of its wild overreaches.
2. New Age understandings have been dismissed because of their overreaches.
3. Classical meditation, as important as it is in locating True Self, doesn't have a real seat at the table in terms of understanding identity.

4. The critiques of separate self being the sum total of identity—which were levelled by the likes of Skinner and Pentland saying, *We're social selves, not separate selves*—are valid but stop short. They don't go far enough.

There's nothing else in the wings. There's nothing else happening.

What did da Vinci do in the Renaissance, at a time between worlds? He told a new story about what it means to be a human being and about the human being's relationship to Cosmos based on the best data available. That's what we need to do now.

> *We need to reformulate, in the most gorgeous, stunning way possible, what it means to be a human being. We need to fully and deeply answer the question, Who are you? We've got to put out a great library. We need serious academic work, and we need serious inspirational work.*

You might think, *Let me write a book and sell a million copies.* That's not going to do it if it's not grounded in powerful, deep, and inarguable First Values and First Principles. These are not inarguable because they're dogmatic. Just as da Vinci did, or as Freud did in his best work, or Einstein did in his best work, or Marx or Darwin sometimes—we are pointing to what is actually, self-evidently true.

So writing a great book, which is just this nice book that people read, and they feel good—*this is such a great New Age book*—is not going to get us there. Or: *let's build another megachurch*; no, that's not going to get us there, either.

**We have to evolve the source code.**

If we don't, then Alex Pentland wins. Look up Alex Pentland. He is a distinguished professor, a good guy whose heart is likely in the right place. I'd love to have dinner with him. But what is he—along with Google, Facebook, WhatsApp, and all the rest—actually doing?

1. It's based on a straight profit mode.
2. It commodifies people: *Let's give you a whole bunch of apps. You're going to be herded based on your data.*

That's a word they actually use: they call it "herding." You herd people, and you create this effective hive, which *determines the rules of acceptable behavior.* And this all may be founded in some good motives. There are always good motives, but **it's also the utter destruction of what it means to be human.**

What does it mean to be human? To be a human being, friends, brothers, and sisters, means to live within the Tao.

## LIVING WITHIN THE TAO

The Tao is *the Way.* **The Tao is First Principles and First Values that are not subject to commodification, First Principles and First Values that are our lifeblood.** They're the axioms and premises by which we live.

They're the self-evident truths that define our humanity:

- Our sense of the irreducible dignity of our uniqueness.
- The sense of Eros that animates us.
- The sense of love that moves us to stake everything on another person, to sacrifice.
- That which moves us to care, to hold another human being.
- That which moves us to heroism.
- That which moves us to search for meaning, and to disclose meaning.
- The building of trust and loyalty between human beings.

- It's how we resolve conflict.
- It's how we feel each other.
- Our yearning for intimacies, which define and animate who we are.
- The dignity of our desires.

## IT'S NOT THAT WE BECOME BAD HUMAN BEINGS, BUT THAT WE CEASE BEING HUMAN

All of the above is completely left out by Alex Pentland. All of it was left out by B.F. Skinner, and his book *Beyond Freedom and Dignity* was attacked because he revealed this position too openly. Alex Pentland is currently rewriting Skinner but doesn't quote Skinner at all. He's doing it much more cleverly. Again, Alex Pentland is not a bad man. He's a good man, but here's the important thing to note:

- It's not that we become bad men. We cease being men and women.
- It's not that we become bad human beings; we cease being human beings.
- In other words, they are articulating a vision that is no longer a *human* vision. It's about what C.S. Lewis once called "the abolition of man," which was the title of one of his major works. We have moved to increasingly conquer nature. And then we conquer human nature. **When we conquer human nature, then nature itself has conquered us.**
- Human nature is to live in the Tao.
- Human nature is to live according to First Principles.
- Human nature is to be animated by First Principles and First Values. We're at this da Vinci moment where we must articulate First Principles and First Values. Everything depends on it.

> *If we can't articulate a new story, then Alex Pentland and the whole gang of well-meaning, Skinner-inspired folks are going to be the ones to define Reality.*

That's where it's heading now.

**The entire enterprise of social media, the entire enterprise of the web, which we're all plugged into and is increasingly defining us**—and even more so our children and grandchildren—**is becoming a mechanized, machine intelligence-guided hive world.**

Reality is not behaviorism. Reality is Eros.

But the entire enterprise of the web is based on "herding" and "tuning" behavior—aka manipulation, but using more pleasant names, with more appropriate, social guises.

So what are we standing for? We are the revolutionaries. That's our job, and I know it's audacious, but it's true. **Our commitment is not just to have a nice experience today but to actually articulate the core structures of the Tao, the Way,** not of one religion, one worldview, not of one system of psychology, but rather it's based on:

- The implicit premises known by human beings.
- The interior intelligence of Divinity animated through human beings.
- The evolutionary impulse in all of its wonder, beauty, and poignancy, animated through human beings.

We're here to integrate the best of that knowing of what it means to be a "baby-faced divine" —a human being animated by First Principles and First Values—and to express those and to codify them in Evolutionary Love codes. **We are doing this not for the sake of conquering the world** but for the sake of making this knowing available so that it becomes part of our very source code, part of the air we breathe—because that's what's getting lost in what we are calling the "tech plex."[1]

## THE QUALITY OF YOUR UNIQUE VOICE IS SACRED

I've been reading this book over the last couple of months called *Surveillance Capitalism*, Shoshana Zuboff. Her critique of Big Tech is gorgeous, but there's ultimately no ground to it because there's no discussion of Eros. There is no discussion of First Principles or First Values. It's all euphemism—some of it is helpful, but none of it clear. There's no rallying point. There's no universal grammar of value, so we can't come home.

One of the things that's currently happening on the web is the hijacking of your voice. **Your conversations and vocal inflections are being analyzed to determine how you're going to act, in order to gain a more effective predictive analysis, not just to sell you things through ads but also to control your behavior.**

*It's a complete desecration of what it means to have a voice.*

A voice is sacred. A voice is not some experience that's hijacked by your digital assistant, Alexa, which is really surveillance capitalism in disguise, seeking to mine data from human experience. **Your unique and gorgeous voice is being used to develop a secret script, a secret text, the machine**

---

[1] By tech plex we mean the technological infrastructure of society, which includes the entire "planetary stack" (Benjamin Bratton's term), as well as the daily immersive environment constituted by social media and the "internet of things." The tech plex is unique in that it has facilitated a new world in which technology is no longer a tool, but an immersive environment. We live inside of that plex. That plex moves all the way up and all the way down the planetary stack. The tech plex is constituted by infrastructure, social structure, and superstructure, as we have previously defined these terms. Clearly, there's infrastructure, in terms of the actual physical structures of the tech plex. There's social structure, in relationship to the laws that govern and the absence of laws in relationship to the tech plex. And third, there's superstructure. That is to say, the technology actually codifies particular values and ignores or bypasses or rejects other values. The tech plex is not values-neutral; the tech plex implies a set of worldviews or superstructures.

**intelligence-generated personality profile of how you'll act—in order to be able to manipulate you.** That's not what voice is. That's not what human conversation is.

- Human conversation is sacred.
- Life is a series of conversations.
- Voice is sacred.
- The quality of your voice is sacred.
- We need your unique voice, your Unique Self.

This is it. We're the revolution. I wish I could tell you there are twenty other groups out there doing this. There aren't. There are people doing individual pieces that are wildly important, like imaginal cells in a chrysalis in which the caterpillar is turning into a butterfly. Of course, the immune system is trying to kill these imaginal cells. They've got to find each other, so we should, of course, find and work with other groups that are doing important things. Of course, there are important things happening, but this piece—this evolving of the source code, this articulation of the memetic structures—is ours to do, friends.

We're working together with our Unique Self Institute, and we're going to be working deeply on this answer to the question of *who are you?* I'm going to interpose this with the writings coming out of the tech world today—from MIT, from Alex Pentland, from Google and Facebook. We need to compare and contrast Unique Self and Unique Self Symphony with these other voices.

Of course, we need to say: *These other voices are not bad people.* **They're not the devil. They just don't have available to them memetic structures—memes, the *dharma*, wisdom from the interior sciences—that are needed to chart the way forward according to the Tao.** So we've got to articulate those source-code structures so that they'll be picked up. If Unique Self Symphony was available as general model, then we could program differently and shift our culture.

## EVOLUTIONARY LOVE CODE: YOU ARE A UNIQUE SELF

The answer to the question "Who Are You?" is: You are a Unique Self.

You are an irreducibly unique expression of the LoveIntelligence and LoveBeauty that is the initiating and animating Eros and energy of All-That-Is, that lives in you, as you, and through you.

Your Unique Self is the expression of your True Self. The total number of True Selves in the world is one. Your awakening takes place when you realize that you are not merely a separate self but a True Self. True Self is the singular that has no plural.

True Self + your Unique Perspective and your Unique Intimacy = Unique Self.

Finally, when you find others to join genius with you, you contribute your Unique Note into the planetary awakening. You are being recorded and activated in the Book of Evolutionary Life.

You become *Homo amor*.

You are lived as a unique expression of *LoveBeauty* and *LoveIntelligence* of All-That-Is.

Your Unique Self—*Homo amor*—joins a Unique Self Symphony, and the planet awakens as love.

Now, we have to unpack every sentence here.

We have to show that uniqueness is a First Principle of Cosmos.

We have to show that the evolutionary quality of uniqueness is actually structural to Cosmos.

We have to show how uniqueness awakens in an individual human being and what that means.

We have to distinguish between Unique Self and separate self.

We have to show why uniqueness doesn't separate, but that it's the currency of connection.

We have to show why the irreducible dignity of every human being is that they've got a unique quality of intimacy, which is not part of hive intelligence:

- They have a unique perspective.
- They have an irreducibly unique way of being and becoming.
- They have a song to sing, and a poem to write, and a story to live that is irreducibly significant. They're not merely separate selves; they're unique expressions of the One.

*I'm not merely True Self* (which is when I've moved beyond separate self), but I realize, ***I'm part of the Field of Consciousness.*** **Then I awaken more deeply to my infinite personhood as Unique Self.**

Where did my Unique Self come from? Reality itself intended it. One of the trajectories, or plotlines, of Reality is the movement to more full uniqueness, more conscious uniqueness. Human dignity is based on the fact that we're not exchangeable cogs, and we're not just acted upon.

Pentland and Skinner write, "We have to realize that we're not the locus of action; we're always being acted upon by the world." No, we act upon the world. If we're always being acted on, then we're objects. It's the ultimate objectification. **But we are not objects; we are creative subjects. All human beings are born creative. The entire Evolutionary Impulse, the creativity of Cosmos, lives in each of us individually and uniquely.**

- Not as separate selves; this is our higher individuation beyond separate self.
- Not our ego self. It's our higher individuation beyond ego. That's my gorgeousness. *Wow!*
- Unique Self is this unique incarnation of *amor*, of the *LoveIntelligence* of the Cosmos.

We're not alone in the Cosmos. We're always held by the Divine, by the Infinity of Intimacy.

Together, all our Unique Selves are faces of the larger Field of *LoveIntelligence*, of integrated Oneness, the unified field of the whole thing of which we're all individuated pieces, gorgeous beyond imagination.

We're not alone. **We're at home in Cosmos.**

## DEEP INWARDNESS IS WHERE WE CREATE MEANING

"We were meant to be here": This is the anthropic principle, which points out the fine-tuning of Cosmos for the emergence of humanity. Our notion of Anthro-Ontology is the principle that says that *deep inwardness is the space where we create and discover meaning.*

For Skinner, Pentland, and many researchers and commentators in the tech plex world, *the inward space of creation of meaning is completely irrelevant.* Instead, *meaning is created by people acting upon us.* That's the assumption, and **the entire web is built to tune and herd us into a benign, effective social unit, which will destroy our very humanity**.

In the end, we become replaceable. When we become replaceable and we're not needed, then we're in utter disaster. **Not only will we have lost our humanity—a form of existential risk—but we become** *irrelevant.*

What happens when we become irrelevant when the issue is not exploitation, as it was in the twentieth century? In the twenty-first century, the issue is that *most human beings in the world won't have jobs* because AI has taken over.

Then at a certain point—and I'm going to add something I've never added before—**we're no longer even needed as customers.**

We're currently needed as customers, constantly targeted by ads, but what happens when AI starts trading with other AIs controlled by a small group of people? That's exactly what's starting to happen. This very tiny elite is controlling the AI world in a world of scarce resources, and human beings are increasingly not needed at all. And of course, in the background you have the threat of climate change and nuclear war—you have all kinds of threats at play.

**What do you think happens to all those irrelevant human beings? It's not good.**

If there's no script of Unique Self engraved in the heart of Cosmos that shapes our policy, if there are no First Values and First Principles animating culture, if there's not a movement towards Unique Self Symphony that shapes our education… then we are headed towards a world in which **most of humanity becomes irrelevant. That's where the threat is, and it's very real.**

We are here to meet it.

We have not yet begun to fight.

We have not yet begun to love.

We have not yet begun to pray.

We have not yet begun to come together as Unique Self Symphony:

- In which the cacophony of human voices comes together
- In which no human voice is lost
- In which every human being emerges together in this larger explosion of Outrageous Love

**That's a force that can sweep away all tyrannies, whether they're ostensibly benign tyrannies with smiles on their faces or more overt forms.**

We're not alone.

So let's end with a prayer. We turn to the Divine and say, *Oh my God, we know we're imperfect. We're imperfect vessels for the light, and we all have holy and broken Hallelujahs.*

Let's pray together as we come before the Divine. All of our personal lives are at play, and they matter immensely. **I just talked a lot about the big picture, but all of our lives in that big picture matter enormously.** Our holy and broken *Hallelujahs* matter enormously because our Unique Selves have unique stories.

*Those stories have dignity, and our needs have dignity.*

# CHAPTER FOUR

# THE UNIQUE SELF RESPONSE TO THE EXISTENTIAL RISK OF THE TECH PLEX

*Episode 224 — January 24, 2021*

### THE HUMAN BEING AS A UNIQUE CONFIGURATION OF EVOLUTIONARY LOVE

*Why are we here?* We are here to make a revolution. We are here:

- To reject the status quo of mediocrity.
- To reject the status quo of superficiality.
- To reject the status quo of averageness.
- To reject the status quo of ordinariness.

We are here to reject the status quo that refuses to embrace the unbearable greatness and dignity of every human being on the face of the planet.

We are here to reject the status quo which doesn't realize that all human beings are not only born equal but are born uniquely creative.

> *The unique creativity of every human being is the essential pillar upon which society is enacted and erected.*

## THE UNIQUE SELF RESPONSE

The fundamental narrative of self is based on the question: *Who am I? Who are you?*

You're an irreducibly unique expression of the LoveIntelligence and LoveBeauty that is the initiating and animating Eros and energy of All-That-Is, that lives in you, as you, and through you, that never was, is, or will be ever again other than through you.

As such, you have an irreducibly unique perspective and an irreducibly unique quality of intimacy that come together to form your unique capacity to give your Unique Gift that's uniquely needed in your unique circle of intimacy and influence.

For that you were born, and that's the source of your joy, and the source of your delight, and the source of that which allows you to be aligned with the evolutionary impulse moving uniquely in you.

That's the ticket for you to join the larger Unique Self Symphony in which you play your unique instrument.

That story of identity is not fanciful, and it's not conjecture. It's the best integration of the deepest validated insights at the leading edge of culture in the traditional, modern, and postmodern periods.

We've taken the best-validated insights and woven them together.

**From that new weaving emerges a new story of identity greater than the sum of any of the previous stories.** It must stand at the center of:

- Every political platform.
- Every economic platform.
- Every social platform.
- Every psychological platform.
- Every tech platform, including biotech and infotech.

> **We have to download that narrative of identity based on the human being as a unique configuration of Evolutionary Love into the tech plex itself—and therein lies our future.**

That is the memory of the future. That's why we're here. The failure to do this is a potential existential risk, in that we become trapped in a world of separate selves in a state of war with each other, which then leads to all of the generator functions of the existential risk, which leads to the very death of humanity, the sixth mass extinction.

However, it may also lead to a second form of existential risk. The second form of existential risk is not the death of humanity generated by all these factors that come from rivalrous conflict and the win/lose metrics success story. This story ignores the narrative of identity that we just laid out, of Unique Self and Evolutionary Unique Self, what we call the narrative of *Homo sapiens* becoming *Homo amor* and the need for the emergence of the New human and the new humanity.

The second form of existential risk is that if we don't embrace, articulate, and deploy this narrative throughout culture so that every child knows as they grow up—

> I'm a Unique Self. I have a story to tell, a song to sing, a way of laughing, loving, and being. I have a unique instrument to play, and that unique instrument is needed by the Unique Self Symphony.

—then we're left with a tech plex whose intent is to extract from us information that's then sold to third parties, who are misaligned with us and our values, in order to manipulate our decision-making process. That is what's called today "the nervous system of the planet." That's the tech plex. The two movements today in society are the constant upgrading of machine intelligence and the constant downgrading of human beings.

And this is not meant to be depressing; this is an incredibly urgent, ecstatic invitation to be revolutionaries, **to stand in the breach and say,** *Let there be light, let there be self*—because that's the true nature of Reality, and to articulate the revolutionary message of Evolutionary Love. We ask the question: *Who are you?* You are an irreducibly unique expression of All-That-Is, that lives in you, as you, and through you, and you are needed by All-That-Is. *Wow!*

The failure to do that is an existential risk of a second kind: not the death of humanity but the death of *our* humanity—a prospect that's equally or even more threatening.

## RECODING THE ALGORITHMIC STRUCTURE OF THE NERVOUS SYSTEM OF THE PLANET

I'm first going to try and set a little bit of the context for this conversation. We're going to begin to see how the principles of the Intimate Universe need to create what I call "digital intimacy." If you look up on the Center for Integral Wisdom website, there are about fifteen subsections, including one called "digital intimacy."

We're just beginning to articulate what that is, and how we need to bring it into the center, because we all live in this digital plex. Those of us who have children or friends or nephews who are "digital natives" get it. We're raising the next generation as "digital natives." They're living inside of the web plex. It has to become not a place of alienation, a place of downgraded humans.

We have to upgrade.

We have to pour Evolutionary Love into the tech plex, into the algorithms.

**We've got to recode the algorithmic structure of the nervous system of the planet with Evolutionary Love and with these new narratives of identity.**

- That is how we respond to existential risk.
- That is how we move from dystopia to utopia, to a joy that's unimaginable, to a freedom and dignity that we can't even begin to dream of.

This happens when human beings come together—both face-to-face and through the "digital intimacy" of the tech platforms—to create Unique Self Symphonies that self-organize and self-actualize Reality to a level of Goodness, Truth, and Beauty, which was the inherent intention of Reality itself.

**Our intention is a Planetary Awakening in Love through Unique Self Symphonies as a revolutionary response to the existential threat**, which not only threatens the sixth mass extinction—the existence of human beings—but worse: our very humanity itself.

## EVOLUTIONARY LOVE CODE: UNIQUE VOICE, PRAYER, AND THE TECH PLEX

The Unique Self is the inward space of uniquely lived experience from which meaning is discovered.

The Unique Self is under attack in multiple ways, including the assumption of Big Tech and Big Data that the human being is no more than a "social" self; the assumption of the spiritual traditions that the human being is either a True Self or an obedient self, and the shared assumption the world over that the human being is only a separate self.

The cultivation of Unique Self is therefore the overriding moral imperative at this moment in history.

Voice has a voiceprint. It's got a pattern. It's a configuration of waves. Unique configurations of pressure waves are the originating uniqueness of Reality itself and the history of the Cosmos. The wave of a unique voice is an expression of this evolution of uniqueness all through Reality—so be inspired.

One of the places where unique voice is expressed most dramatically is in prayer. It's why we don't pray silently. We pray with our voices, and when we can't use our voice, we write. Interior prayer is beautiful, but one of the things that the great traditions, the interior sciences, understood is:

> *It's critical to speak our prayers, to articulate or write words, because that brings them to a new level of Reality and to a new dimension of impact.*

There's an enormous amount of brain science research happening now. My colleague Bessel van der Kolk at Harvard, who's a close colleague of one of our board members, Lori Galperin, wrote a book called *The Body Keeps the Score*. It's a great book, and it has a section on the neuroscience of writing. We have both the neuroscience of writing and the neuroscience of speaking, which show that when feelings get translated and expressed, something deep happens.

We're about to go into prayer… so what is prayer?

**Prayer is the affirmation of the dignity of first and second person, not only third person.**

In some sense, the tech plex is all based on the reduction of the human being to third-person "it" experiences, like processes and systems. Third person means "I" view "you" as an "it," so let's call that "I/it." Those are "I/it" relationships. That's third person.

## THE EXISTENTIAL RISK OF TECHNOLOGY

In fact, the CEO of Microsoft, Satya Nadella, said in 2017, "We've now gotten to a place where the human being becomes a first-class object on the web."

That means: We analyze everything we can about what we know about the human being based on their track record on the web.

We take all the information available about a human being, and we grind it through machine intelligence. That gives us a personality profile, and then we can use that. We can sell that information to a third party, who will then use that information to determine, impact, and potentially change what your course of action might have been, essentially robbing you of your genuine freedom of decision-making and influence, beyond your awareness.

In other words, **a human being becomes an objective, an object. The human being is no longer a subject.** We then gather all your information through machine intelligence—your breadcrumbs, as it were, your digital exhaust. That's called your "behavioral surplus." That's then fed into machine intelligence.

Just so you get the depth of this, Microsoft had a program that could tell whether you'd get a particular disease in twenty years based on how you typed. Machine intelligence is incredibly, exponentially powerful and able to invade your self—both consciously and unconsciously—to create this shadow text about you that you don't have available to you.

That's the classical third person perspective.

---

*Prayer instead emerges from the first and second person. "I pray" means there's a depth of me that's underneath that third-person objective part of me. I pray not for my object self; I pray for my subject self, for my radical, infinite subjectivity, the quality of value that is me.*

---

## THE UNIQUE SELF RESPONSE

That's the quality of first person that lives in you.

Then there's the second-person quality. We talk to the Infinite Intimate as we all talk to each other—as second person, that which lives in the space in between.

In the great mystical literature they talk about Krishna and Radha, that space in between, that's where prayer happens.

Prayer is not third person. Prayer is the first person of Reality having a "you" experience, your irreducibly unique expression of intimacy and value, your name. Your name then reaches for the divine name. That quality of personhood lives through Cosmos.

**The tech plex has reduced Reality only to third person. That's the objectification of Reality, the disqualification of the universe.** Of course, Reality is third person, but it's also first person and second person. That's where prayer happens.

Prayer's not a dogma or superstition. Yes, there are superstitious, mythic versions of prayer, which we need to move beyond, just like there are mythic versions of science we need to move beyond. No, God is not a cosmic vending machine, which you put in a quarter and get a desired result.

Prayer is the unique first person of my unique configuration of intimacy, turning to the Field of Intimacy, to the second person, the Infinity of Intimacy, and saying:

> *Oh my God, I know you, and you know me. Hold me. I need you. You manifest in me. You generated me, and I turn towards you, who is Source to me, and I say hold me and help me because I can't do it myself, and I turn towards the Infinity of Intimacy that, quite literally, knows my name. Wow!*

I ask for everything—but not everything my ego self thinks it needs. I don't ask for a candy bar or some superficial increase in status.

I ask for my deepest heart's desire.

> *Prayer affirms the dignity of personal need because I'm a unique expression of the personhood of Cosmos.*

None of that, my friends, as it stands now, is available in the tech plex. None of that is available in the algorithms. We need to recode both our own interior algorithms and the algorithms of what Alex Pentland of MIT calls the "nervous system of the planet."

**We need to recode the nervous system of the planet with first person and second person. That's why we need prayer.**

So let's pray now. Let's pray as unique personhood, as Unique Selves, as unique qualities of intimacy, and turn to the God that knows our name.

Turn to the Tao that knows our name, turn to Essence that knows our name, turn to the Infinity of Intimacy that knows our name—and ask for everything. That's where Leonard Cohen's coming from when he talks about the holy and the broken *Hallelujah*. He's talking about the dignity of personhood turning to the Infinity of Intimacy and crying out, *Hallelujah*.

*Hallelujah* means, *Oh my God, the pristine gorgeousness of gratitude for being alive.* And it means the drunken intoxication, the brokenness of it all. The holy and the broken *Hallelujah*, which is the full quality of personhood, reaches towards Source to the Infinity of Intimacy and says, *I'm going to put all of it at your altar. Will you receive me? Will you hold me more tenderly, more fiercely, with more Eros, with more joy, with more yearning, with more raw aliveness than I've ever been held before?* Let's be in our hymn together, the holy and the broken *Hallelujah*, with Leonard Cohen.

We bring these prayers together, tie them like a bouquet of roses, and we offer them to the Infinity of Intimacy, who gathers them up, blown open by their fragrance, and responds to each name individually, personally, and intimately.

Barbara and I were deep in this conversation on Unique Self and Unique Self Symphony, this understanding that all persons are born creative. This is the vision that we're holding together.

## A REVOLUTION OF SELF: RE-"SELF"ING

So we're at a moment of revolution, and the revolution has to be a revolution of self, a "re-selfing."

**Self has been disqualified in three fundamental ways.**

1. The Western notion conceives of the human being as merely a separate self, a skin-encapsulated ego locked in rivalrous conflict with every other separate self, each one governed by their own win/lose metrics in zero-sum games against each other.

This notion of separate self is a generator function for existential risk.

It drives the exponential growth curves. It drives the extraction economy. It drives all the forms of fundamental status and power conflict, which lie at the root of the global intimacy disorder.

2. The second notion of self that, as revolutionaries, we have to reject is the notion that currently drives the tech plex: We are only "social selves." A person is the sum total of their social cues and is totally defined by social pressure.

This was the worldview of the key architects of the tech plex that animate Google, Facebook, and all the rest. This is why the web is built on a series of social cues that are directed against you, misaligned with your fundamental will, and stealing your attention, which you so desperately need in order to cultivate your deeper and more authentic sense of personhood and self.

3. We have to reject what's called in the Enlightenment traditions the True Self, the realization that I am one with, inextricably identified with, the larger Field of Consciousness.

We have to reject the True Self, but not because the True Self is wrong. **The True Self is true but partial, just as the social self is true but partial, and just as the separate self is true but partial.** Each have their own dignity. None of them will take us home because each of them by themselves fails to capture who we truly are.

When we weave together, in the ultimate revolutionary act, which is the act of "re-selfing," we realize that we are not merely separate self with its important dignity. We're not merely social self with its important understanding, and we're not merely True Self, the one self of Enlightenment. We are Unique Self.

Unique Self means you are an irreducibly unique expression of the LoveIntelligence and LoveBeauty that is the animating energy and Eros of All-That-Is, that lives in you, as you, and through you, that never was, is, or will be ever again other than through you. As such, you have an irreducibly unique perspective and an irreducibly unique quality of intimacy that come together to forge your unique capacity to give your Unique Gift to your unique circle of intimacy and influence. Your gift is needed by All-That-Is.

By giving your gift, you are playing your instrument in the Unique Self Symphony.

*No*, we say to the tech plex, *we're not merely part of a social hive superorganism.*

*No*, we say to the old Enlightenment traditions, *we're not merely absorbed in the One where uniqueness disappears.*

*No*, we say to the superficial readings of social contract theory, which animate the West, *we're not merely separate-self citizens.* We're all of those, but we're so much more.

## THE UNIQUE SELF RESPONSE

- We're irreducibly gorgeous, unique configurations of Eros, intimacy, and desire.
- We're Unique Selves.
- We're moved by the vocational arousal to respond to the call.
- We're personally addressed by Cosmos itself.
- We're needed by All-That-Is.

That's the core of the revolution, and that realization is cause for a new social movement. It's cause for the most important response to the social hive, which is the death of our humanity.

The response is a Planetary Awakening in Evolutionary Love through Unique Self Symphonies in which each person fully knows this: *I've got a song to sing. I've got a poem to write. I've got a way of being, laughing, loving in the world that's uniquely mine, and it's needed by All-That-Is.*

Let every child know this.

Let every human being be animated.

Let our hearts and souls dance to this inner gorgeous truth of Reality, which blows us open with joy, with invitation, with purpose, and with Eros.

# CHAPTER FIVE

# RE-SELFING THE HEART OF THE COSMOS: ACTIVATING UNIQUE SELF AND UNIQUE SELF SYMPHONIES

*Episode 225 — January 31, 2021*

### WE ARE A BAND OF OUTRAGEOUS LOVERS, REVOLUTIONARIES WHO ARE EVOLVING THE SOURCE CODE

If we really get this, how can we not cry tears of joy, tears of a broken heart, tears of longing, and tears of trembling before She as we realize that She needs our service?

*Avodah tzorech gavoha:* Reality needs our service. Reality needs your service. And we need each other as a band of Outrageous Lovers coming together literally as revolutionaries.

If you want to get a sense of the feeling that animates One Mountain, Many Paths:

- It's not a fundamentalist religious feeling, although there's value in that.
- It's not a human potential movement or New Age feeling, although there's value in that.
- It's not an intellectual, political podcast, although there's value in that.

The feeling is revolution. Think of a café in Paris during the Enlightenment or in St. Petersburg as Marxism was spreading. Marxism was missing so many critical pieces, so it devolved into Communism, which was incredibly destructive, but there was this moment of potential. I want to get this straight with you because this is going to be the piece we're going to talk about today.

Communism is utopianism without First Principles. Communism is this grand utopian vision intended to actually shift Reality. It's a cosmocentric vision, but what is it missing? It's missing First Principles.

Reality needs your service. The name of the Divine, in the deepest reading of the interior sciences, is the name of every being that ever was, is, or will be—inscribed together in the name of God.

*If one name is missing from the name of God, the name of God has no power. We're all part of the Divine name.*

It's so deep. That's a First Principle and a First Value of Cosmos.

Communism was utopianism. It was a move to an actual cosmocentric consciousness:

*First, I'm going to be world-centric. I'm going to feel the whole world, and I'm going to feel that the whole world needs to be changed, and I'm responsible for changing it, and I'm going to take responsibility for the whole thing.*

That's called utopianism. That's gorgeous. But Communism was utopianism sans First Principles and First Values. So we're at a moment today where **we need to take responsibility for the whole thing**.

What's the energy animating us? The energy is: *We're a band of Outrageous Lovers. We understand that we live in a world of outrageous pain, and the only response to outrageous pain is Outrageous Love.*

We live in a world of outrageous beauty, and the only response to outrageous beauty is Outrageous Love.

Outrageous Love is not ordinary love.

Outrageous Love is not mere human sentiment.

Outrageous Love is not a strategy between two separate-self egos.

*Outrageous Love is the current of Reality itself. It's the heart of existence itself.*

Outrageous Love is Eros, Reality is Eros, and Eros has expressions as intimacy, as desire, as radical uniqueness, as creativity, and as personhood.

These are First Principles and First Values of Cosmos that evolve from matter to life to mind to the human world, and then they evolve through the human world. **These are not just** *eternal* **First Principles and First Values; these are** *evolving* **First Principles and First Values.**

We must articulate these First Principles and First Values and bring them together with a utopian vision, meaning a vision of moving from *Homo sapiens* to *Homo amor*. *Homo sapiens* is the old vision of the human being, which has been downgraded and degraded. We've begun to understand the human being as this hyper-small, separate self engaged in rivalrous conflict governed by win/lose metrics.

The narrative, the plotline, is a success story that's become the animating narrative and story. That animating narrative and story is the source of the existential risk to our very humanity, and which may cause the death of humankind:

- Through the extraction model.
- Through exponential growth curves.
- Through the widening gap between haves and have-nots.
- Through rogue actors with access to exponential tech.

- Through a whole list of issues, which then contribute to climate change, to the nuclear threat, etc.

**This false narrative, this story of the old human and the old humanity, this broken *Homo sapiens*, is the root cause of existential risk, which is literally the death of humanity.**

This failure of narrative is leading not just to the death of "humanity," which is the first form of existential risk, but also the death of "our humanity," which is the second form. It's not that human beings will disappear, but we'll stop being human as we understand human beings to be. And that's the direction we're moving in.

So what we're asking is, *Who are we?* We are a band of Outrageous Lovers who are revolutionaries.

The energy that animates us is—think, again, back to our café in Paris or St. Petersburg—it's Marxism. But Marxism is without First Values and First Principles. **Marxism assumed that the Cosmos is purely material and run only by the forces of the techno-economic base.** All those forces are enormously important, and Marx's insights are critically important. They're part of the story. Marx didn't understand that there's actually *Value* in Cosmos underneath the material structure of Cosmos.

---

*Value means First Values and First Principles. Value is irreducible. Value is not deconstructable. The dignity of the individual human being has ultimate Value.*

---

You can't tinker with or remold society without alignment with the First Principles and First Values of Cosmos that evolve and appear uniquely in us. We have to be in alignment with those First Values and First Principles.

The single most important thing we can do today is to reclaim them, but to reclaim them is not to claim something that was once clear. It's actually to *evolve*, to articulate a new vision of First Values and First Principles because that vision has gotten lost. It's been lost, and it's never been fully and appropriately articulated.

**Our context is revolution.**

We want to blow our hearts open.

We want to be inspired. We want to be breathed by Outrageous Love itself.

We have a revolutionary vision, which is to enter into the source code of what's happening, understand it, and diagnose it—because diagnosis is the first stage in being able to transform and to heal.

We need an accurate diagnosis, and then we need to articulate the new set of memes, the new story that becomes the animating plotline of a global ethos for a global civilization.

This is necessary because the failure of story, the failure of narrative of self, is the source of existential risk, whether that's the death of humanity or the death of *our* humanity (which are two forms of existential risk).

**It's only by evolving and articulating a new story based on the best-validated insights of premodern, modern, and postmodern thinking that we can respond to that existential risk.**

## WE NEED A NEW STORY OF VALUE, GROUNDED IN FIRST PRINCIPLES AND FIRST VALUES

We can't heal where we are today; we can't respond to existential risk, we can't respond to a world of a broken source code without **articulating a new source code**, new memes based on First Values and First Principles, which are:

- A new narrative of identity.

- A new universe story.
- A new narrative of power.
- A new narrative of desire.
- A new narrative of communion.

At the center is the *dharma*, the First Values and First Principles that are the basis of the new set of narratives and that will become the matrix for an ethos of global civilization.

In that sense, I just want to say that *our entire system says no to the guru model*. In the guru model, there is a person whom God moves through and is the source of authority. We utterly say *no* to that.

We also utterly say *no* to the San Francisco New Age model: *We're all just getting together and talking, and we're all just friends on the path, and everyone's opinion is equally valid, and let's just make sure that we're listening deeply and reflecting back to each other.* No, we're not doing that either.

*There actually is a dharma—not everything is equal, and not all ideas are equal.*

We've spent twenty-five years trying to work through and **integrate the best set of validated insights from premodern, modern, and postmodern wisdom**. We're putting forth a set of ideas, and they're completely challengeable, but you've got to challenge them, not just say, "I disagree."

You've got to say, "Okay, wow. I've looked at all the theories of self, and there are seven reasons why we need to adjust it this way," and we'll get to that in a moment.

We're a Unique Self Symphony creating this *dharma* together, and anyone who wants to step in—*to step in "for realsies"*: step in and study and open their heart and practice and participate at the table in actually evolving the source code—is welcome. Step on in. Everybody's welcome.

## EVOLUTIONARY LOVE CODE: THE UNIQUE SELF IS THE INWARD SPACE OF UNIQUELY LIVED EXPERIENCE FROM WHICH MEANING IS DISCOVERED

**Part one:** The Unique Self is the highest integration of the leading-edge values of traditional, modern, and progressive thought. The emergence of Unique Self takes the unique value propositions of each of these three great stages in the evolution of consciousness, which is the evolution of Love, and weaves them together in a new emergent of Love, which is precisely what we have called *Homo amor*.

**Part two:** The Unique Self is the inward space of uniquely lived experience from which meaning is discovered. The Unique Self is under attack in multiple ways, including the assumption by Big Tech and Big Data that the human being is no more than a social self, the assumption by spiritual traditions that the human being is either a True Self or an obedient self, and the shared assumption the world over that the human being is merely a separate self. The cultivation of Unique Self is therefore the overriding moral imperative at this moment in history.

We're going to focus on the second part of the code, particularly: *The Unique Self is the inward space of uniquely lived experience from which meaning is discovered.*

That's a big sentence.

Unique Self is under attack in multiple ways. Maybe a better way to say it is *the Unique Self needs to be articulated* because the current assumptions of self, the narratives of self, are all fundamentally downgraded.

1. We've got the narrative of Big Tech and Big Data, which I want to unpack. No one understands that Big Tech and Big Data are operating from a particular narrative of self, which I would call the "social self," which assumes one's identity is entirely defined in relation to others.

2. The assumption of the Enlightenment spiritual traditions, which say, *No, you're a True Self,* means you're one with the all, but actually, *you've got to move beyond your personal story.*
3. The third assumption is that you're an obedient self. You're obedient to your religion or to your tradition. Again, that can be partially true if you're operating within a particular tradition, but that's not what the self is at its core.
4. Pretty much everyone assumes that the human being is some version of a separate self: *I am a discrete, hyper-individualized human being.*

None of those models work on their own, and tragedy comes from these partial, fragmented, fractured notions of self, each of which comes from a particular moment in history.

We have to integrate the best aspects of all of those **because each one has a spark of the holy. Each one is true but partial. We integrate them, weave them together, and something new emerges much greater than the sum of the parts.** What emerges is this new activation of self, this "re-selfing" at the very heart of Cosmos. It's the emergence of Unique Self as a process of "re-selfing."

That's what we need to be doing, but **it's got to be soaked in, rooted in, intoxicated with the very heart of Cosmos itself.** The Universe feels, and the Universe feels love. The Universe doesn't feel ordinary love; the Universe feels Eros, Outrageous Love, *amor.* It's an Amorous Cosmos; an Intimate Universe, and **intimacy and *amor* are not human creations**.

---

*The human being expresses uniquely— at whatever their developmental stage is, at higher and higher levels of consciousness—this quality of amor that is inherent to Cosmos.*

---

**That's the good news: it's not a reductive, materialist Cosmos.** It's not *a tale told by an idiot full of sound and fury, signifying nothing.* The good news is that the Universe is a Love Story, and your story and my story are chapter and verse in this Love Story.

**It is an Amorous Cosmos, and that's why we know the revolution is going to succeed.** *Wow!* But how long will it take, and how many tears will be shed along the way? That depends on us.

## THE FIRST PRINCIPLES AND FIRST VALUES OF PRAYER

What are the First Principles and First Values of Cosmos that prayer is based on? There are about four or five of them. A First Principle and First Value means *you locate it inside,* or *you go inside to the deep, inward space of meaning.* You get quiet, and you access First Principles and First Values that live in this inward space of meaning. We call this Anthro-Ontology: *It lives inside of you.*

- Then you realize that those First Principles and First Values currently live all across the world and throughout all stages of human history.
- Then you realize that there's even earlier versions of them that live in the pre-human world of life.
- Then you realize they live even in the world of matter and more fundamental forms.
- Then you realize that these First Principles and First Values animate Reality itself, and that they evolve at each stage.

So what are the First Principles and First Values of prayer?

1. The first one would be personhood. Prayer is based on personhood. What does personhood mean? It means that Reality is not just third person; it's not just "objective" external systems and objects. Reality is not just first person,

which is my own inward experience of self. It's also second person, where my first person meets your first person and a new space in between is formed.

Prayer is based on Reality not just being exteriors. Reality is also interior. Interiors are a First Principle, and one form of interior reality is personhood—**there's a personal quality to Cosmos**. I have an experience of my own interior—which means that I can be joyful, suffer, and make meaning—and my interior also yearns for your interior. That's personhood.

The personhood that lives between us is not just "you and I"; it's not just two separate selves. That personhood *participates in the Field of Personhood*.

If the human being doesn't have the experience of *my interior or finding the interior of another human being*, I'm devastated.

Remember the movie *Cast Away*, with Tom Hanks? He's stuck on an island after his FedEx cargo plane crashes on a beautiful, tropical island. He's learned how to survive. He's mastered the elements of the island. He can live there by himself forever, but at one point he decides to risk his life, with a ninety-nine percent chance of death, as he casts himself into a makeshift raft on the sea *because there's no other human inwardness to meet his inwardness.*

*There's no other personhood to meet his personhood.*

This First Value of personhood goes all the way up and all the way down. Personhood lives at the human level, and personhood evolves through all the stages of human consciousness. But **there's already personhood at the level of life, in the world of animals, and there's a good argument to be made that there's also a dimension of interiority and personhood in the world of matter.**

That's what Alfred North Whitehead, the mathematician who wrote *Principia Mathematica* with Bertrand Russell, talked about with his notion of **"prehension," the proto-interiority that lives in the allurements of the atomic world.**

What are some other First Principles and First Values upon which prayer is based?

2. This notion of inwardness, which ultimately generates unique personhood, is also a First Principle and First Value of Cosmos. It's not just me, meaning **my personhood participates in the personhood of the whole thing**. My personhood is not generic. There's not just a field of generic personhood. So it's not just that consciousness has a personal quality, but that **I have *unique* personhood**.

3. There is the First Principle of intimacy: Personhoods want to come together. There's a fundamental movement in Reality to move from separateness to integration, from alienation to integration, from being a part to being part of a whole—without losing my own individuality. That's the movement to intimacy, which is the movement of Reality. **Reality is evolution, and Reality is the evolution of intimacy.** The movement of intimacy is the movement to create new shared identities, whether that's between subatomic particles, between galaxies, or between human beings.

Are you beginning to notice these First Principles and First Values?

So how do they work in prayer?

**In prayer, I realize I'm a unique quality of intimacy that never was, is, or will be ever again. Therefore, my uniqueness is dignified, and my personhood is dignified, which means that my needs are dignified.**

Prayer affirms the dignity of personal need: *I desperately want to be held, and I want to be received.* That desperation to be held and received is not a pathology.

- It's a beautiful desperation.
- It's a sacred desperation.
- It's the desperation with which Rumi wrote love notes to

Shams, and Shams wrote love notes back to Rumi.
- It's the Outrageous Love notes that birth Reality itself.
- It's this wholly gorgeous desperation to find shared identity.

Importantly, we never exhaust this intimacy with only one person. Underneath and beyond any individual personhood—because it's never dependent on one person—there's a Field of Intimacy and that Field of Intimacy is personal.

We call that field the Infinity of Intimacy, while other people may call it God. God means not *that which is other or alienated from Reality*, not some cosmic vending machine. No, **God is the aliveness of Reality that is both beyond the personal in the sense of personality but** *also* **the infinitely alive Personhood of Reality**.

Then we begin to realize: the personhood that lives between us participates in this larger Field of Personhood, and just like you can hear me talking, and I can hear you talking, the Infinity of Intimacy can hear us talking.

**So when we pray, it's intimacy seeking intimacy.** It's me or you as a unique quality of intimacy turning to the Field of Intimacy itself that holds us, that knows our name, and we say:

> *Oh my God, hold me, help me, love me, enter me, penetrate me, caress me.*
> *Can I tell you what I need?*
> *Can I please tell you what I desperately need?*
> *Will you hold me, will you help me, will you love me?*
> *That's prayer—and it's a realization, not a dogma.*

We're going to pray now, and we're going to invite Leonard Cohen in his hymn, both the holy and the broken *Hallelujah*.

Leonard Cohen is bringing lineages together. He's doing something in his body. He's bringing together his own Eros and his own confusion, but he's also bringing together in that gorgeous confusion deep lineages of second person and first person. He practiced deep within the Western tradition of Hebrew wisdom. Every week, he practiced, and he got this notion of *turning to the Infinity of Intimacy that knows your name.*

What's the reason this song has more covers than any other song? What's the reason this song is played everywhere around the world? Both the Democrats and the Republicans each played it at their respective conventions and gatherings. Why?

Because it expresses the second-person quality in Cosmos.

People are attracted to the song, and they're not even quite sure why, but:

> *This is a shared place beyond polarity where we're all reaching for the Infinity of Intimacy.*

We're all realizing that we are each unique qualities of intimacy and that we want to hold each other. We yearn to be held. The Intimacy of the Universe is a First Value and First Principle beyond the polarities. **And the way to get beyond polarity in politics today is to begin to articulate the fundamental First Values that lie beyond and beneath the polarities.**

# CHAPTER SIX

# GOD NEEDS YOUR SERVICE: THE GREAT DIVINE RISK, THE FIRST PRINCIPLE OF UNIQUE SELF

*Episode 226 — February 7, 2021*

## THE CHOICE IS OURS: WE CAN EITHER DESTROY OURSELVES OR BECOME A MODEL FOR LIFE IN THE GALAXY

We are coming together from around the world in this moment in which the effects of cascading injustice and cascading inequity are flaring up all over the world. And yet we're also at this moment of innovation, this moment of feeling that something new needs and wants to be born—and can be born.

At this moment of massive existential risk to our very existence, which rages in different forms around the planet—the ultimate dystopia, the end of existence, quite literally, no future—we often turn away because it's too much. **Yet it's not just dystopia that lurks at the door; it's also utopia: an unimaginable vision of human dignity, of humans in the entire natural world living together, an emergence of not just human beings but all life in the Cosmos finding each other.**

I don't know how many of you have noticed, but until about 2017, the entire topic of extraterrestrials was off the table.

Since 2017, it's now been put back on the table. It was originally on the table between 1942 and about 1955 very intensely. Then, for a number of reasons, it got taken off the table intentionally by the governments around the world. Now, it's back in a very big way. *The New York Times* has written a series of major stories about the topic. *The Washington Post* and other mainstream media are actually reporting and validating that extraterrestrials seem to be, by all accounts, real. That's real.

We've known in the great traditions that the Cosmos is teeming with potential life. That's a beautiful expression. What that means—a new possibility in a galactic universe—is critically important. If you track how we began to hear and feel signals from beyond this universe, it began with World War Two around 1942, and especially with Los Alamos, with the first nuclear weapon tests.

These first nuclear tests seemed to give rise to the first attempts at contact, and the first reports of receiving contact also began then. There's an entire industry of movies about this, and many major figures in the music industry who talk about their own encounters. There are serious figures, like John Mack from Harvard, who have written extensively about the topic. **The notion of a galactic universe is important. It speaks to new potentialities for the human being that are unimaginable.**

Just like our nuclear explosions put the eyes of the galaxy on us for the first time, our capacity to take our humanness and transmute it into a utopia—to have *Homo sapiens* evolve and become *Homo amor*—will also attract the best of the galaxy to us. The way we evolve is no longer just a question of human beings on planet Earth.

If you situate yourself in the Cosmos—and I've talked about this several times in the last two or three years just briefly—and examine the evidence for larger fields of galactic life, it's enormous. Again, it's entered into mainstream conversation for many reasons that are beyond the purview of this conversation.

## GOD NEEDS YOUR SERVICE: THE GREAT DIVINE RISK

**Our capacity to access the leading edges of intelligent and loving life around the galaxy is deeply related to our own ability to evolve from *Homo sapiens* to *Homo amor*.**

We become the strange attractors towards a better future. We become the forces of allurement.

So we live in a CosmoErotic Universe, which is filled with love, with Eros, and with life in multiple forms. It's an incredible moment we're at. We can either destroy ourselves, and destroy the future, and not participate in the explosion of life in the galaxy, or we can become a leading-edge model for life in the galaxy, showing what life could be and what life might become.

### THE STORY OF HUMANITY IS GOD'S GREAT RISK

The story of humanity is God's great risk. Divinity's great risk is the story of life, and it's the story of the human being on planet Earth. Will that risk be fulfilled?

*The divine Lover, who loved us so much that She/He breathed us into existence for the sake of intimacy and for the sake of the evolution of intimacy: will that risk be realized as the grand and gorgeous adventure of spirit, which ultimately evolves to an unimaginable utopia?*

Or will people be too afraid to stand for justice, too afraid to stand for integrity, too afraid to stand for goodness, too involved in their own comfortable spiritual activities but unable to see the whole picture, unable to take their Unique Risk, unable to speak truth to power, unable to step out of the bourgeoisie and become spiritual revolutionaries?

That is to say: *We want to upend the degraded structures of Reality and put new structures in their place*—but gradually, carefully, fairly, justly. Wow!

It's a moment in time unlike any other with its threats and challenges, with its potential for utopia and dystopia.

The response is to evolve the source code.

The response is to tell the new Evolutionary Story:

- The new story of the movement from *Homo sapiens* to *Homo amor*.
- The new story of Self.
- The new story of desire and the dignity of desire and the divinity of desire.
- The new story of need and the dignity and divinity of need.
- The new story of the evolution of love.

Friends, it's the single most important work we can do in this generation.

It's the moral imperative for every single one of us.

It's not happening in some university or in some intelligence agency.

It's happening right here.

We are invited—nay, not even invited—we are *demanded* by Reality. Anyone who's here is self-selected, has self-chosen. We're family to each other. We're not biological family; we're Evolutionary Family. We're a band of Outrageous Lovers.

**We're spiritual revolutionaries. It's not about the socioeconomic system, but about the energy of being committed to transformation—** not to the sudden transformation but to the gradual transformation, to the introduction of new First Values and First Principles that articulate a new shared Story that becomes the matrix for a global ethos for a global civilization.

Are we ready to put ourselves on the line, to take our Unique Risks, to access our deepest heart's desire, and to participate uniquely in the evolution of love, in generating a Planetary Awakening in Love through Unique Self Symphonies?

## EVOLUTIONARY LOVE CODE: YOUR UNIQUE GIFT ADDRESSES A UNIQUE NEED

> Your Unique Gift addresses a unique need within your circle of intimacy and influence that can be addressed by you and you alone.
>
> In that precise sense, your Unique Gift is needed by All-That-Is.
>
> In this precise sense, *you* are needed by All-That-Is.
>
> Reality—God—needs your service.
>
> Your deed is God's need.

Your Unique Gift addresses this unique need. What is the sense of need? We're going to discuss need and Unique Self. This is super important and super beautiful, but we can't do it unless we're soaked, intoxicated, and alive with the very feeling of Cosmos itself.

**Yes, Cosmos has a feeling.**

No, that's not a fundamentalist idea. We don't go fundamentalist here. It's not a New Age idea, or a traditional idea, or even a progressive idea. **It's actually a fact of Reality.**

This is a post-postmodern realization. It's an integration of the leading edge of all the sciences: both the exterior and interior sciences.

The essence of it is, if I can use the ancient formulation from the *Song of Solomon*: *Tocho ratzuf ahava*, "Its insides are lined with love." *Amor, Amor, Amor.*

Love.

It's not ordinary love, but Outrageous Love.

We live in a world of outrageous pain. That's true, and we're never going to turn away. The only response to outrageous pain is Outrageous Love.

We live in a world of outrageous beauty, outrageous truth, outrageous goodness, and the only response is Outrageous Love. *Wow!*

**Outrageous Love is not ordinary love. Ordinary love is a strategy of the ego.**

I was talking to someone a couple of days ago, someone I love dearly, but my heart is broken that they're turning away from justice. My heart's just completely broken, but I've got to get beneath ordinary love, which is an exchange contract. It was a person I felt betrayed by in a fundamental way. Sometimes, you've got to hold it, and sometimes you've got to walk away. So let's just love outrageously.

This is a moment for loving outrageously, meaning we love from the heart source code of Cosmos itself. The one heart of Cosmos, which generates Reality, is *Amor*—its insides are lined with love. And love begins at the very inception of Cosmos.

---

*Outrageous Love or Evolutionary Love incepts Cosmos, animates Cosmos, and is cause for the evolution of Cosmos.*

---

I had the delight of penning a short essay that Ken Wilber and I put together in a book called *Your Unique Self*. There's a little essay at the end called, "Evolutionary Love," which was the birth of this next stage of teaching and *dharma* and the memetic codes we're doing. Then, in 2014 we spent an enormous amount of time articulating the vision of Outrageous Love. It's unbelievably important. Outrageous Love is my true nature. In other words, I participate in the Eros or the Outrageous Love or the Evolutionary Love that moves Cosmos itself.

This is not some small idea. It's not, *Okay, I get it, I know that. I've heard that before.* No, it's huge. **The desire—a quality of Eros—that moves in me is the desire that moves Cosmos.** My truest appetite that makes me most hungry is the hunger of Cosmos itself. The urge, the pulse, the throbbing that moves through me is the urge, the pulse, and the throbbing of Cosmos itself.

> *Some people say desire is the root of all evil. In fact, shame is the root of all evil. Desire is actually the root of all goodness, truth, and beauty. But it's not just any desire. It's clarified desire, my deepest heart's desire. That is the root.*

*Who are we?* Factually, based on the best interior and exterior science: **We are unique configurations of intimacy.** We're unique expressions of Outrageous Love

We're held, always, by the Infinity of Intimacy. The Infinity of Intimacy holds us. It's the Personhood of Cosmos.

## FIRST PRINCIPLES AND FIRST VALUES OF COSMOS: THREE PRIMORDIAL PERSPECTIVES

The three primordial perspectives are First Principles and First Values of Cosmos. What are the three primordial perspectives?

First person, *it lives in me.* So Sartre, even after he rejected all value, said, "I've got to assert the dignity of the first-person voice." It's a primordial perspective of Cosmos, first person. It's my experience of myself. It's a unique quality.

When I really get my great "I," when I go all the way home with my great "I," I realize, *I am.*

My first-person voice participates in the voice of Divinity. I'm a unique expression of the divine voice—I'm unborn, I never die, and I'm completely continuous with consciousness, but *my first-person experience is that voice living in me in its unique expression.* That's first person.

Third person is, *I look at all the people: this person, and that person, and that person,* those are all third person. *We're describing him and her and they and them, the populations of the world.*

Then second person is that place of personhood between us. It's the reason that in the movie *Cast Away*, Tom Hanks throws himself into the sea on a makeshift raft with a five percent chance of survival at best. *When I don't have another interior subjectivity to meet my own, when there's not a second person to meet my eye, then life feels valueless.*

It's not good to be lonely. All of the good of Cosmos is nullified by the intensity of the loneliness and the alienation. So second person liberates us from alienation. That's love. That's love in the second person, God in the second person.

These three perspectives are values of Cosmos. It's not a cosmic vending-machine god, not a god owned by one tribe, not a god who's just the abstract forces of Cosmos. No.

**All the forces of Cosmos, which are divinely animated**—the third-person Eros that animates all of Reality, all the laws of physics, all the laws of mathematics, all the four fundamental forces, all of the grandeurs of Cosmos in all of its infinity, in all of its complexity, in all of its exponentialized magnificence and brilliance, all of that through all the hundred billion galaxies—**all of it is sitting in a chair, looking at you, knowing your name, desperately wanting to be in intimate communion with you.**

That's God in the second person. That's the Infinity of Intimacy, and it's the Infinity of Intimacy we turn to in prayer. What do we ask for? We ask for everything. We turn to the Infinity of Intimacy, and we bring our holy and our broken *Hallelujah*.

# CHAPTER SEVEN

# FROM THE HUMILIATION OF NEED TO "YOUR NEED IS MY ALLUREMENT"

*Episode 227 — February 14, 2021*

### SETTING OUR INTENTION: RECODING THE SOURCE CODE IN ORDER TO BE AT HOME IN REALITY

We're evolving the source code of consciousness and culture. That means that we're trying to recode Reality itself in order to be whole, in order to be alive, in order to experience joy, in order to be at home in Reality, in order to be madly in love for real in a way that lasts and deepens, and in order for the world not to self-destruct as we stand in this moment poised between utopia and dystopia, confronted by two major forms of existential risk.

The first form of existential risk is the potential death of humanity—physical extinction of the species as a plausible possibility.

Steven Pinker got this wrong in his chapter on existential risk in his book, *Enlightenment Now*. He didn't crunch the numbers, and he sidelined the possibility. He got it wrong. Toby Ord wrote a great book a few months ago called *Existential Risk*, which I would read as a response to Pinker's *Enlightenment Now*, which tells the classic "good news" story.

There are great dignities to modernity, of course, but existential risk is so potently real on so many levels.

So that's the first existential risk: the death of humanity. The second kind of existential risk is the death of *our* humanity. They're intimately linked with each other.

We've talked about how we respond to that existential risk with enormous joy as storytellers—but it's not a fanciful story, conjecture, or a made-up story. Instead, **we come together and realize that the core of the breakdown, at its very essence, is a failure of story, a global intimacy disorder, which blocks global coherence.** Every single form of existential risk is global in its nature. That's a big sentence.

> *There are no more local problems. Every problem is global. Every form of existential risk and most forms of catastrophic risk are global.*

Therefore, it can only be responded to through global coherence, through concerted global action, coordination, and cooperation. **But you can't get to cooperation if you don't have a shared Story. You only have a shared Story if you have a set of First Principles and First Values that unites us, and that comprises a shared vision of Reality.** It's a big deal. Without that, there's no game. It doesn't even begin. Articulating a new shared Story is critical. I'm just setting our intention:

- We're here with radical joy.
- We're radically alive.
- We're delighted beyond imagination because we're engaging in the great revolutionary, evolutionary act imbued with the very love that animates Cosmos itself in telling the new story based on First Principles and First Values that then become the matrix of a global ethos for a global civilization.

Oh my God, what an insane privilege.

# THE EXISTENTIAL RISK OF TECHNOLOGY

## OUR DEEPEST EXPERIENCE OF LOVE POINTS TO THE EXPERIENCE OF COSMOS WITH ITSELF

We've finished two books on this recently, which are 150,000 words each. We finished most of it before Barbara Marx Hubbard passed, and we spent the last year and a half completing different dimensions of it. We show what it means to realize from a scientific perspective, using both exterior science and interior science, that **we live in an Amorous Cosmos, that we live in *The Universe: A Love Story*, and that we live in an Intimate Universe**. That's the core of our Universe Story, which includes:

- A story of identity
- A narrative of community
- An economic narrative
- Narratives of governance and education

But I want to focus not on the deep science and the enormous amount of sources we cited from every different discipline. I want to just say it really simply, so we can get this because this is Valentine's Day. Let's find each other. I just want to say it in the most simple way.

In the depths of simplicity, it's like this:

Imagine the person you feel most connected to: it might be a son, a daughter, a brother, a sister, a beloved, a friend, someone you know now, or someone you knew at one particular time. **Find the person, or maybe two people, whom you feel completely, madly, absolutely connected to, where the love connection is strong and alive and potent and powerful, and feel it coursing in you.**

So here's the second simplicity. It's the most beautiful, elemental, pointing-out instruction.

*What binds you to that person?* That's love. That's Eros. The realization that emerges from all of the exterior sciences at their leading edge integrated with the interior sciences is:

The very same feeling of love that binds you to that person "for realsies"—you'd give your life for it; you'd give up everything to make that love deeper and more real, to protect that person, and just to have a moment with that person. Being with them makes you feel at home in Cosmos—**that very same experience that you have with that one person is the experience of all of Cosmos with itself.**

---

*It is the love that literally binds all of Reality together in mad love with Itself and with each other in every moment.*

---

That's not a metaphor, or a simile, or a conjecture, or poetic reach. That's not a spiritual idea or religious dogma—that is the nature of Reality itself validated by the leading edges of all the interior sciences through the generations. Oh my God.

This is why, my friends, **it's only when we fall madly in love that we actually feel at home in the Universe.**

Krishna and Radha together in the Hindu pantheon, Shiva and Shakti, God and Goddess, the upper waters and the lower waters, the zero and the one, they're yearning for each other—not just in love but *madly* in love.

That's what Rumi says: *love madly*, love insanely—**because that's the nature of Reality itself.**

Happy Valentine's Day, everyone.

## EVOLUTIONARY LOVE CODE: IF YOU ASK, YOU MUST SURELY NEED; YOUR NEED IS MY ALLUREMENT

If you ask, you must surely need: your need is my allurement.

**Need is the evolutionary driver of Cosmos.** Cosmos responds to need. Cosmos dignifies need.

Take the notion of natural selection, which, by the way, is but one sorting mechanism that organizes the process of life leaping forward, and there are five or six other major evolutionary mechanisms, from symbiosis to horizontal gene transfer, etc. The old, now discredited notion that evolution happens only through natural selection and random mutation, and that's the sum total of evolution—is nonsense. Perry Marshall wrote a great book called *Evolution 2.0*, in which he goes through the literature and brings together the nonsensical notion that evolution is simply random mutation. Random mutation, like in engineering, is noise by itself; it's only one dimension.

So what is evolution? **Evolution is the process of love in action.** Evolution is real. Evolution is absolutely real; evolution is the process of love in action. Evolution = love in action. Evolution is Eros unfolded.

**Love responds to need, to authentic need**—which is why it's so important not to claim to need something that you don't.

## COSMOS IS A LOVE STORY, AND LOVE ALWAYS RESPONDS TO GENUINE NEED

To clarify your needs, to know what you truly need, is everything.

To know what I need is, in some mystical traditions, the essence of prayer. Prayer, for example, in one original Semitic language is *Palal*. *Palal* means "to contemplate," meaning prayer is an act of contemplation. What are you contemplating? *What do I really need, but for real?* When I really need it, I ask for everything.

**Prayer affirms the dignity of my clarified personal needs. And when I own the dignity of that need, in some sense, Cosmos responds.**

Sometimes Cosmos responds in a way that's exactly aligned with what we wanted Cosmos to respond. Sometimes Cosmos doesn't. Sometimes Cosmos responds in mystery. *But Love always responds to need one way or another.*

Cosmos is a love story. It's an Amorous Cosmos. In an Intimate Universe, love always responds to genuine need. So:

- You've got to claim your need.
- You've got to own your need.
- You've got to claim your genuine need with pride.

I was talking the other day with a dear friend of mine who mentioned in passing, "Well, who wants to ask people for money?" I'll just tell you a little secret. I have no trouble ever asking anyone for funds to keep the Center for World Philosophy and Religion going because I know we're going to change the source code of culture. It's a privilege. It's about when you really know that it's genuine, it's authentic.

Whether it's:

- A need to be touched or held
- A need to be adored
- A need to be needed
- A need to be chosen
- A need to be desired
- A need to be recognized
- A need to be intended

These are all core human needs, so *I've got to claim the dignity of my need. I have to respond to all of those unique needs in my unique circle of intimacy and influence.*

## IN PRAYER, GOD SAYS, "YOUR NEED IS MY ALLUREMENT"

That's what prayer is. **Prayer is when we turn to God—the God who's not merely the Infinity of Power.** The god you don't believe in doesn't exist. It's not the caricatured, cosmic vending-machine god. **It's the God in first person, second person, and third person.**

- The God that lives in me.
- The God that holds me.
- The God that is the Eros.
- The God that drives and animates the four fundamental forces in all of Cosmos.

We turn to God—particularly in that face of second person, the Infinity of Intimacy—and we say: *Oh my God, I love you and I need you, and here's what I need.*

God's so madly in love with us, that God says to us: *Your need is my allurement.*

When we really ask, when we ask with everything we have, God says: *If you ask, you must surely need.*

And Divinity in some way responds.

**Let's be very clear. There is mystery in Cosmos.** Divinity responds billions of times, and there are times when we can't hear the response. **Sometimes the response is not even in this lifetime.** That's true, but we know as a fact of Cosmos—based on methodological, empirical research exhaustively done, for example, by Ian Stevenson and his colleagues—that *it's not over when it's over.*

We know that we reincarnate, and when we do, we can reincarnate from one world to another world. We were in this kind of world; now we're in a completely different kind of world. You really get that the atmosphere of your current life matters much less than you think.

- It's a journey of completion.
- It's the soul's journey of fulfillment.
- It's your Unique Self's journey of mad wholeness, which is the great gift of Cosmos.

## THE PRACTICE: PRAYER IS ALWAYS IN SOME WAY HELD, AND HEARD, AND RESPONDED TO

Let's turn to the Infinity of Intimacy that hears every word. Just like we hear each other—intelligence in us hears each other—the Field of LoveIntelligence hears us.

No prayer goes unanswered.

The answer is sometimes different—sometimes it's more discernible, sometimes less so—*but no prayer is ever in vain.*

*Prayer always shifts and impacts and transforms, and is in some way held, and heard, and responded to.*

So when we pray, let's ask for everything, and clarify our needs, and ask in a way in which Reality has to respond. *Your need is my allurement* because I'm standing in the dignity of my needs for the sake of the Whole.

We bring it together, friends. We take the flowers and the petals of these prayers—we quite literally raise them up, and we impress them on the lips of the Divine.

Oh my God, amen. *Thank you, thank you, thank you for the most gorgeous prayers*, says She, says He, says we. Oh my God.

## "YOUR NEED IS MY ALLUREMENT" RESTORES THE DIGNITY OF NEED AND EVISCERATES SHAME

Your need is my allurement. What does that mean?

We all have a fundamental experience in that we're shamed when we're trying to get our basic needs met. Maybe I'm worried that I don't have enough money to pay my bills. Maybe I'm worried about my bank account in a fundamental, survival way. **I'm humiliated because it feels like a violation of my dignity that I should have to actually struggle simply to survive.**

Human beings have struggled to survive throughout history, which is tragic. It's one of the reasons I'm in favor of universal basic income. Of course, it has to be done in a way that doesn't destroy the motivational architecture of society, and people do have to give back.

There has to be a clear set of contributions, and it has to be monitored and evaluated. But no one should feel like, *Oh my God, I can't pay my rent. Where am I going to go?* It's painful.

We all have basic needs for nurturance, for nourishment. There are different levels of being nourished, and in some sense they're all included in Maslow's Hierarchy of Needs. But beyond Maslow, there's a second, deeper hierarchy of needs, which are the core human needs:

1. I have a need to be recognized.
2. I have a need to be chosen.
3. I have a need to be intended.
4. I have a need to be not just loved, but adored.
5. I have a need to be desired.
6. I have a need to be needed.

All of those needs are basic rights of the human being; they are all ways in which we are touched.

**We have a need to be touched:**

- Emotionally
- Spiritually
- Existentially
- Psychologically
- Creatively
- Physically

Those are erotic needs. The baby reaches for the mother's breast or the bottle, and the baby yearns for the mother's arms. We're all babies. In some sense, we never outgrow that.

One of the most beautiful things is when my son Zion, before he leaves the house, comes to get a hug. He does it very low-key, but he won't leave the house without getting his hug because we all need that hug. None of us wants to leave the house without getting a hug, and none of us are home without the hug. But what happens is:

- Sometimes the hug's not there.
- Sometimes there's a lack of attunement.
- Sometimes it doesn't show up the way we need it to show up.

That's what we mean when we say *we're humiliated in getting our basic needs met*. Later in life, when these needs are recapitulated:

- When I need to pay rent, but I'm not sure I have enough money.
- When I need to make a living, but I'm not sure how to do it.
- When I need Eros and physicality, and need to be touched in all the ways, but I can't get those needs met.

When this happens, I'm humiliated again. It recapitulates the original humiliation I experienced. **I re-experience my original humiliation as a child in getting my needs met.** That's the source of one primary form of toxic shame: the inability to get my needs met and the humiliation I experience in getting my needs met.

## THE SHAME IN GETTING MY NEEDS MET CAN BE HEALED IN THE SEXUAL

Where is this healed? **The place where this is healed**—when possible—**is in the sexual.** You only ever have to do it once, and you can access the healing.

> *In the sexual, in its most beautiful form, we move from the humiliation of our basic needs to our beloved feeling—crying out, incarnating the truth—that your need is my allurement. It's very powerful.*

It doesn't matter whether you're sexually active now—maybe it happened once in your life—but you can access it, and you've got one experience of that enlightenment. You might not have realized what was happening then, but you can go back to the memory now—and when you go back to the memory, then it's happening *right now*.

You have this moment when you're locked together, like the cherubs above the Ark of the Covenant in the Holy of Holies—Solomon's Jerusalem Temple. The cherubs are in sexual embrace above the Ark of the Covenant, and the voice of the Divine emerges from between the two cherubs. It's so beautiful.

Why are the cherubs in sexual embrace? Because it's in sexual embrace when you have a need. *Touch me that way. Hold me that way.*

Guide your beloved: *This is the way I need to be touched. This is the way I need to be aroused. This is the way I need to be held. This is the way I need to be loved.*

And your beloved says to you in the deepest way: *Your need is my allurement.*

**When you hear your beloved say to you, *your need is my allurement*—and it just has to happen once—the dignity of need is restored.**

The early humiliation of basic needs is healed in this core and gorgeous way.

- This is so huge.
- This is a fundamental of Cosmos.

- This is cash, not credit. If you get this, you literally change inside. This is the cash *dharma* of Cosmos.
- This is the inner structure.

## WE PARTICIPATE IN THE ALLUREMENT OF REALITY, AND WHEN THAT ALLUREMENT IS BROKEN, WE HAVE A DESPERATE NEED

Reality is allurement.

Reality is allurement all the way up and all the way down.

We participate in the allurement of Reality.

When that allurement is broken because we feel like we're not attuned—perhaps because a parent, or an early caretaker, or a teacher, or culture at large, can never be fully attuned to us, and not that they've done something wrong—we have this desperate need.

**Need is holy. *Authentic* need is holy.** *Berur*—the clarification of need—is the essential human action. *So we need to clarify our needs.*

A baby's needs are very clear. The baby knows:

- I need to be touched.
- I need to be held.
- I need to be nourished.
- I need to suck at the breast of the nursing mother, who is the incarnation of the Universe: A Love Story.

When those needs are humiliated, when that attunement is broken, when that allurement is short-circuited, then *I'm fundamentally humiliated at the core of my being*—not because it's a bug in Cosmos but because we always fall away. It's the nature of Cosmos: we always fall away.

But after we fall away, we recover.

Recovery is not the solution to an accident; recovery is the intention of Cosmos.

Recovery is not a bug in Cosmos but a feature of Cosmos.

**Sexuality heals.** And sexuality may be what we classically refer to as sexuality, or it may be just being held in another person's arms. It may be a sustained experience of our lives, and it might be an experience that's fleeting and ephemeral. I can even experience it in self-pleasuring.

**I can experience my need, and I dignify that need.**

I hear Cosmos whispering in my ear as the Beloved: *your need is my allurement*, and shame is healed.

# CHAPTER EIGHT

# IF YOU ASK, YOU MUST SURELY NEED: YOUR NEED IS MY ALLUREMENT

*Episode 228 — February 21, 2021*

### SETTING OUR INTENTION: HUMANS ARE *HOMO IMAGINUS*

One Mountain, Many Paths is a revolution. That's what it is at its core. The energy is revolution and evolution, the deep understanding that *we're willing not to look away*.

We're willing to engage Reality.

The primary crisis in Reality today is not a crisis of resources, but a crisis of imagination.

Step 1: We're willing not to look away.

Step 2: We understand that it's not a crisis of resources; at its core, it's a crisis of imagination.

In the original text of one of the lineages, the first human being is Adam. Adam's not a man; Adam contains both the masculine and the feminine, so it's the full human being. The word "Adam" actually means "ground" as in human or *humus*—the ground, the earth.

But the word Adam has a second meaning: *adameh*, which means "to imagine."

> *We are all Adam. That is to say, we are Homo imaginus: we are creatures of imagination.*

And we're talking here about the new human. We're talking about the evolution from *Homo sapiens*—who operates based on rivalrous conflict and win/lose metrics—to *Homo amor*—to the human being who incarnates evolutionary intimacy.

## HOMO AMOR ACCESSES HIS/HER UNIQUE OUTRAGEOUS ACTS OF LOVE THROUGH IMAGINATION

*Homo amor* realizes that:

*You are an irreducibly unique incarnation of the LoveIntelligence, and LoveBeauty, and LoveDesire that is the initiating and animating Eros and energy of All-That-Is, that lives in you, as you, and through you, that never was, is, or will be ever again other than through you.*

*And as such, you have unique, Outrageous Acts of Love to commit.*

Reality is Eros, and Eros is the animating force that drives Reality. Eros is the animating force that animates the four physical forces of the Cosmos. Eros can be called Evolutionary Love and Outrageous Love, but these are the same force. It's not ordinary love, not the love that's thrice exiled to the human being:

- We exile love from the Cosmos itself, and we apply it only to the human world.
- Then we exile love from most of the human world, and we apply it only to just a few humans.
- Then with those few humans, we exile love to only very particular experiences of either romantic or parental love,

and everyone else is out of the circle of love and intimacy.

That's ordinary love. **Our love lists are too short, my friends**.

We're talking about Outrageous Love, which is the initiating and animating Eros, the Outrageous Love of All-That-Is, that lives uniquely in me, that speaks uniquely through me.

*Who are you?*

This is no declaration, no New Age claim, no fundamentalist claim. At your core, based on the leading edges of the interior and exterior sciences across premodern, modern, and postmodern thought, integrated in a new wholeness, a new emergent, is the realization that **you're an Outrageous Lover**.

That's actually who you are. That's what's coursing through you. You're an irreducibly unique expression, a configuration of intimacy, a configuration of Outrageous Love.

*As an Outrageous Lover, what do I have to do? As an Outrageous Lover, what do you have to do?*

You have Outrageous Acts of Love to commit.

*What do I need to do in order to access them?*

You need to be able to imagine. **You need to be able to imagine the crisis in our lives as a crisis of imagination. You must not turn away from your unique circle of intimacy and influence.** You must not turn away from the larger Reality.

*Where can I commit my Outrageous Acts of Love?*

You have to engage that imagination.

Step out of the yesterdays that determine today.

Step out of limiting beliefs.

Step out of contraction.

Step out of the clench and find the joy.

So here's our intention. Are we ready to imagine? Imagination's everything. My colleague, Yuval Harari, talks about "core values." But ultimately, he says those are figments of imagination, mere imaginings. Of course, this is not his original idea. It comes from Feuerbach, who says, "Wow, God is a figment of our imagination." **Yes, it's true that God is a figment of our imagination, but we forget:** *Our imagination is a figment of God.*

That is to say: The quality of imagination is, for all of the great traditions, the quality of the awakened human being. It's the quality of the Prophet.

- It's through imagination that I access spirit.
- It's through imagination that I access the Divinity that resides in me.
- It's through imagination that I find all that's good, and true, and beautiful.

So, friends, in order to be *Homo amor*, we have to realize we're also *Homo imaginus*.

Who's willing to engage the crisis of imagination in their lives? Because all of us have a crisis of imagination.

Are we willing to reimagine how we understand ourselves?

Are we willing to confess our greatness, to run faster, to be deeper, to be more beautiful, to be more audacious, to be more kind?

Are we willing to let ourselves out of our box? And let everyone out of their boxes—my wife, and my husband, and my partner, and my friend, and my brother, and my sister, and my son, and my daughter, and my mother-in-law? Let's reimagine.

This is the question: *Are we ready to play a larger game?* Are we ready to reimagine? Are we ready to be more than we've ever been before? Are we ready to give ourselves permission to imagine, to give ourselves permission to be excited, to give ourselves permission to be evangelical?

What does evangelical mean? We're sharing the good news.

What's the good news? The good news is that the old caricatures of spirit don't work—they're dogmatic.

The good news is the old dogmas of scientism are equally fundamentalist and dogmatic. We can do the hard work—with blood, sweat, and tears—and integrate and tell the new story. Oh my God, that is wildly, insanely exciting, and at the core of it all is the realization that we live in an Amorous Cosmos.

## SEEKING INTIMACY IS A FEATURE OF REALITY EVOLVING THROUGH US

What we're doing here in One Mountain is reclaiming love as religion—the original love impulse—but we're actually not regressing. We're understanding love and Eros much more deeply. We're bringing to bear the best sciences, the most serious sociology, the best anthropology, and all the schools of psychology—in order to realize that *it's not a declaration*.

In fact, the most accurate universe story we have is that **we live in an Intimate Universe and the Intimate Universe lives in us**. From quarks that come together to form subatomic particles, drawn together by allurement, to subatomic particles that come together to create a new shared identity as an atom, and all the way up the evolutionary chain—Reality is the evolution of love.

Evolution equals love in action responding to authentic need.

If you ask, you must surely need: your need is my allurement.

Everyone knows that we seek intimacy. What we're understanding now in the leading edges of science, both interior and exterior, is that we all seek intimacy.

That seeking of intimacy brings us into the arms of our beloved friend; it brings us to seek the interior of another person and makes us feel like it's not good if we're lonely. All of the good of Reality is canceled in the experience of non-intimacy because we're not alienated from Reality.

> *The fact that we seek the intimate is not a bug in our system, or a pathology. It's an inherent, fundamental feature of the system.*

At the core of the post-postmodern new Universe Story is the realization that "Reality is the progressive deepening of intimacies."

**Reality is not just a movement from simplicity to complexity. Reality is the progressive deepening of intimacies.**

Step 1: Reality is evolution.

Step 2: Reality is the evolution of intimacy.

If we recognize that this is not a placebo idea, not just some sweet thing to say, we'll see this is the best understanding we have of all of the information available in Cosmos at this moment in time. Wow. Reality moves from bacteria to Bach, from mud to Mozart, from quarks to culture, and that movement is the progressive deepening of intimacies. The intimacy that I seek in my life participates in the evolution of intimacy.

Reality seeks intimacy, and we all participate in this movement of Reality.

Do we understand together the dignity that this understanding gives our lives?

**When we're desperately seeking intimacy, it's actually *Reality's desire to seek intimacy through us*.** When we achieve intimacy, it means we create a deeper shared identity.

When I achieve intimacy with the split-off parts of myself, I have a shared identity with the split-off parts of myself. When I create shared identity with the split-off parts of myself, and they can no longer hijack my life, it's a big deal.

When I create shared identity with other people in my life, especially if they're part of my Evolutionary Family, my seeking of intimacy is the movement of evolution—the evolutionary impulse—awake and alive in me.

The old traditions were about "Crush your ego." That's not going to get you home, and it never works. Of course you should be aware of your ego acting out, but you can never crush your ego.

What you have to do is instead *align with the evolutionary impulse*. The evolutionary impulse is way beyond your narrow, separate-self ego and when I align with the evolutionary impulse, two things happen.

The first result is that **I become uniquely creative**. All human beings are born not only equal; all human beings are born uniquely creative. When I align with the evolutionary impulse, I feel a unique pulse and surge of creativity moving through me, and I realize I've got a unique creativity that the world needs.

The second thing that happens when I align with the evolutionary impulse is that **I feel the movement towards intimacy, towards contact, towards touch**—to be touched emotionally, spiritually, physically, existentially, psychologically, and intellectually. We want to be touched in all ways, and we *want* to touch in all ways. That's the authentic and profound nature of Reality—because Reality itself is the Intimate Universe. If we want to find the fragrance and the breath of spirit, we realize that God is not only the Infinity of Power. God is the Infinity of Intimacy.

So at this moment, we turn to that Infinity of Intimacy to pray. This is not prayer as a premodern cosmic vending machine idea, but prayer as the uniquely intimate human being—the Unique Self—whose unique configuration of intimacy is turning to source, turning to the Infinity of Intimacy that knows my name, that breathes in my ear, that holds me intimately—because there are times when we live lives of quiet desperation, but friends if you are awake to the true nature of Reality, *there is never lonely desperation because we are never alone.*

**We're always intimately held by the Infinity of Intimacy that knows our name.**

That's not a dogma. It's not a claim.

It's the deepest scientific understanding of the nature of Reality, this quality in Reality which is:

- First person: It lives in me, in my own "I" experience.
- Third person: The laws of physics, mathematics, and Eros that drives Cosmos.
- Second person: The personhood of Cosmos itself, which is a First Principle and First Value.

All these qualities of personhood are qualities intrinsic to Cosmos, and they participate in the ultimate personhood because Cosmos has a personal face that knows my name.

That's what we mean by God. God is the Infinity of Intimacy that receives and holds my holy and my broken *Hallelujah.*

*Doesn't matter what you heard. There's a blaze of light in every word. The holy and the broken Hallelujah.*

## STORY: THE BAAL SHEM TOV—"IF YOU ASK, YOU MUST SURELY NEED"

Here's the story. It's a gorgeous story, and the story is not about information, it's about invocation. It's one of my favorite stories from deep within the mystical tradition.

## IF YOU ASK, YOU MUST SURELY NEED

There's a man, Moishele, who comes one Sunday morning to the Baal Shem Tov, the Master of the Good Name. The Baal Shem Tov loves holy beggars, but this one looks more broken than anyone. The Baal Shem Tov asks him, "Why are you so broken, my friend? You get to be a beggar. You get to ask for alms, and have your hand out, and your heart can be open. Why are you so broken?" Then the Baal Shem Tov says, "You don't even need to explain." He looks deep in his heart and says, "You lost all of your money. You were a wealthy man, and you lost all of your money three years ago, didn't you?" The beggar is shocked. He says, "How did you know?" The Baal Shem Tov says, "Oh, I can see it written in your soul. I see your pain and your suffering, and I want to tell you that there's a way to get your money back."

Moishele is shocked. He says, "You're right, it was three years ago, and how can I get my funds back?" The Baal Shem Tov says to the beggar, "Do you remember? It was on a particular sacred day of fasting, and you were in the place of worship and prayer. Everyone was fasting, and during the fast you don't eat or drink, but you're allowed to be revived by fragrance, by smell. As is the custom in that lineage, you had a fragrant snuffbox."

The Baal Shem Tov, the Master of the Good Name, says to this beggar, "You went around, and you offered all the people a little fragrance. They would breathe in the fragrance, and they would be revived in the middle of this difficult fast. However, in the back of the house of worship, there was a beggar. The beggar's name was Yankele, and you didn't bother to go back to him. You troubled yourself with everyone else, but you didn't bother to go and give him a pinch of snuff. Yankele has all your money. The wheel of fortune turned and you became the beggar, and now he has all your money, but you can get your money back." The beggar says in astonishment: "How? How could that possibly be? How can I get my money back?" So friends, open your hearts. Open my heart. Let's open our hearts together.

The Baal Shem Tov says, "Go to him and ask him for a pinch of snuff—he now has the snuffbox. He took your money, though not intentionally. The wheel of fortune turned, the karma shifted. He has your money, and he's now taken your particular vocation. He holds the snuffbox. So if you go to him and ask him for a pinch of snuff, and he says, "I'm too busy now," then he'll have done to you what you did to him. The wheel of karma, the wheel of fortune, will turn again, and all of the funds will go back to you."

So Moishele travels back to the town where Yankele used to be a beggar and who now has all of his funds, and he thinks to himself, "Okay, this is going to be easy." He knocks on the man's door at midnight, bangs on his door. Yankele comes to the door, and he's a little sleepy, and he says, "Well, what can I do for you?" He says, "I need a pinch of snuff right now." Yankele looks at him, and he sees him, and he says, "Ah, if you asked, you must surely need." He goes and gets the snuffbox, and he gives him a pinch of snuff. The holy beggar Moishele is devastated. How could this be? But he says, "Okay, I'll get him another way."

Yankele has this tradition where every week, he goes with his family to a tavern where he eats. It's a special time. So you know what happens. Moishele waits at that tavern, and when he's sitting there eating with his family, he bursts in on Yankele, and he says, "Yankele, I need a pinch of snuff right now." Yankele looks up surprised, and he says, "If you ask, you must surely need."

Then a third time, a fourth time, a fifth time, at all of the most inconvenient times, Moishele bursts into Yankele's life and says, "I need a pinch of snuff." Every time, Yankele looks at Moishele, his eyes ablaze with Outrageous Love, and he says, "If you ask, you must surely need."

Finally, Moishele can't take it anymore. He's willing to try his most desperate gambit. This is a desperate moment. Yankele is marrying off his daughter. It's this most precious time, and there's a particular custom. When a man marries off his daughter, there's a particular moment where he does a special dance with his daughter. In Yiddish, it's called a *Mitzvah tantz*. It's the most beautiful, intimate moment between father and daughter before she passes on to the next dimension of her life and enters into holy matrimony. So Moishele slips into the wedding, and right as they're in the middle of the *Mitzvah tantz*, right as they're in the middle of that special holy dance, Moishele interrupts and says, "Yankele, I need a pinch of snuff."

Yankele's naturally taken aback and looks at him. He stops the dance and says— say with me, friends, what does he say?—he says, "If you ask, you must surely need," and Moishele can't take it. He faints and falls to the ground. When they revive him, Moishele tells Yankele the story that the Baal Shem Tov told him, how three years ago on the fast day, when Yankele was still a beggar, Moishele hadn't gone back to give him a pinch of snuff.

Yankele remembers this and understands what happened. He says to Moishele, "I'm going to give you half of my wealth, and let's be brothers together." And in fact, historically, that's what happened. Yankele and Moishele lived together in this town, and poor people from all around the region would come to this town because they knew this was a place where *If you ask, you must surely need* was alive and well and beautiful and gorgeous.

## YOUR NEED IS MY ALLUREMENT

Here's the important thing: people didn't take advantage of this because **when you truly honor need, people go inside and they find their deepest need**. They clarify their desire and their need. "If you ask, you must surely need."

So what is Yankele saying to Moishele? He's saying to him, "Your need is my allurement." Can we feel that together? "Your need is my allurement."

We're all humiliated in some way or another. This word "attachment theory" has shone a light on the importance of our early attempts in life to get our basic needs met. Martha Nussbaum wrote a book called *The Language of Emotions*, a stunning tour de force where she gathers the information on the humiliation of basic needs, though she doesn't use these terms. Of course, Winnicott, Bowlby, and others have talked about this in great depth in their own ways.

It's one of the great revelations of the century: *When I can't get my basic needs met as a child, I'm humiliated.* That humiliation is recapitulated whenever *I can't get my basic needs for being held, for being touched, for being nourished.* We heal that humiliation throughout our lives because *that humiliation's not a bug in the system; it's a feature.*

**One way we heal it is in sexuality.** In sexuality, we experience the rawness of our needs. When our beloved moves in ecstasy, and urgency, and ecstatic urgency to meet our needs, and says to our urgency, *Your need is my allurement*, then the sexual heals that original humiliation when the context of the sexual is sacred.

We know that the sexual models Eros. That is to say, we live in Eros. In all of our lives, the sexual models Eros. This means that **in every dimension of our lives, we say to our beloved, "Your need is my allurement."** That doesn't mean surface needs, and it doesn't mean you get anything you ask for. It means that when you come to me with your authentic need—and that need is a real need, and I can meet that need—then I say to you, "Your need is my allurement."

Oh my God. That's what we say to each other, my friends. Your need is my allurement beyond imagination.

Here are the words of Solomon. We're going to spend one minute chanting it, and then we're going to explode into our dance party. Here are the words. It comes from Solomon himself in the *Song of Solomon*. Solomon from the ancient temple in Jerusalem, home of the Ark of the Covenant. Solomon writes, *Sham Eten et dodai lach*, "Here, I place my love for you."

Your need is my allurement.

If you ask, you must surely need.

Here, I place my love for you.

# THE TAO THAT CAN BE CODED IS NOT THE TAO: EVOLVING HUMANITY BEYOND ALGORITHMS

*Episode 229 — February 28, 2021*

### TELLING A NEW STORY ROOTED IN ETERNAL AND EVOLVING VALUES

Every solution that can address global challenges of existential risk today requires political will. Political will can only be generated from the matrix of a new story:

- A new story that is not fanciful or mere conjecture, but rather a new story that is rooted in Value.
- It's based not in socially constructed values but rather eternal values.
- Eternal values doesn't mean preordained, unchanging values. It means intrinsic values that live in Cosmos and evolve.
- Love is not a social construction; Eros is not a social construction. Eros means the movement of Reality towards ever greater wholeness and ever deeper contact.
- Eros evolves because evolution is the evolution of love.

This is so important, and this is not a human potential movement statement, a fundamentalist statement, a faith assertion, or a New Age claim. No. Based on the best integration of the interior and exterior sciences that we have—spanning premodern, modern, and postmodern thought, across all wisdom disciplines—we can say the following: **1) Reality is evolution, 2) Reality is the evolution of love, and 3) the evolution of love means evolution equals love in action responding to authentic need.** Wow.

Imagine a world in which that is the source code of Cosmos. Imagine a world in which that's the algorithmic knowing that lives in every human being. It's actually beneath all algorithms because it can't be measured—and that's what we want to talk about today.

Today we're going to talk about that which is immeasurable, and we're going to talk about how we experience the Story and how the traces of this Story—the traces of Value, the plotlines of Reality—make us human beings when we experience them. They also define the very nature of Cosmos. We're going to be taking a huge leap forward in articulating that new story today.

Our intention is to tell the new story and to speak it in a way that activates political will. Importantly, the political is always associated with value.

---

*Value arouses political will, and the violation of value arouses political will.*

---

So, for example, the American Revolution and the French Revolution were based on an understanding that there was an intrinsic value in Cosmos that was being violated by the old order of royalty and aristocracy. That experience of the violation of intrinsic value aroused these revolutions. Of course, intrinsic value is often articulated by those who don't have a language for it; it just remains in them from earlier generations. Marx is an example of that.

But let's make no mistake about who we are: we are a band of Outrageous Lovers. And Outrageous Lovers means something very specific:

- We're becoming.
- We're being.
- We're becoming and being the New human and the new humanity.
- We've crossed over to the other side.

That's who we are. That's what we're here for. We're not here for *oh, let's have a nice, sweet, saccharine, and lovely time…* That's beautiful, of course, and there are lots of places for that. And we're not just here for everyone's individual, personal transformation—which is beautiful and necessary and important and part of the transformation of the whole—but **we want to be aware that we're participating, committed, and responsible for the transformation of the** *whole***.**

> *We are political revolutionaries. Our politics is a politics of love, and we're reclaiming religion as love. We're bringing religion and politics together in the highest possible way.*

So if you're up for that:

- If you're up for being a political revolutionary;
- If you're up for taking your seat at the table;
- If you're up for being more excited than people tell you is politically correct to be excited;
- If you're willing to be more audacious than is allowed in polite company;
- If you're willing to access that sense that you've got something to do, that you're needed by Cosmos, and that your deepest

heart's desire matters and is a contribution to the very heart of Divinity—

—then oh my God, we are ecstatic that you're with us. If you have no idea what we're talking about, we're also ecstatic that you're with us. We're just delighted to be together, and we are in total joy in this revolution, even as we're in outrageous pain.

**We live in outrageous pain; we respond with Outrageous Love. We live in outrageous beauty; we respond with Outrageous Love.**

All of it is tinged with laughter out of one side of our mouths, and tears out of the other.

## EVOLUTIONARY LOVE CODE: TO THINK WE HAVE STEPPED OUT OF THE TAO IS THE GREATEST EXISTENTIAL RISK OF ALL

There are two core existential risks.

The first is the death of humanity.

The second is the death of *our* humanity.

The death of our humanity begins when we think we have stepped out of the Tao. We all live in the Tao, always.

To actually step out of the Tao is impossible, but to *think* we've stepped out of the Tao is, in many ways, the greatest existential risk of all—to become disconnected from that sense of being in the Tao.

The god you don't believe in doesn't exist. The cosmic vending-machine god—who's homophobic and belongs only to one nation, and to whom you give a quarter as prayer and get out some worldly good—that god doesn't exist. Don't worry about that god, that god doesn't exist.

But there actually is a Reality to Spirit, and let's call that Reality the Tao.

# THE TAO THAT CAN BE CODED IS NOT THE TAO

*The Tao is the intrinsic quality of Value that inheres in all of Reality, and that intrinsic quality of Value can't be spoken.*

The Tao that can be spoken is not the Tao.

The Tao that can be measured is not the Tao.

The Tao that can be coded is not the Tao.

But words and code and measurement can point towards the Tao.

You can write a love letter, but that's not the Tao, it points to the Tao. We stretch words to their breaking point to point towards the Tao.

One of the words that points towards the Tao is intimacy.

**When we're intimate—with truth, with each other, with beauty, with goodness—our lives incarnate Evolution in person.** The best trajectory of our lives—the successful life—is a life which is a *progressive deepening of intimacy*.

**A successful life equals the progressive deepening of intimacy.**

Can we feel how beautiful that is?

Now, this doesn't mean that I'm having more sex or not. Sex, in its best form, is a form of intimacy. But lots of expressions of sex are non-intimate.

I want to be intimate with truth. I want to be intimate with other. I want to be intimate with all the split-off parts of myself. I want to be intimate with wider and wider circles of knowing, of caring, of doing.

**Intimacy means I have a larger *shared identity* beyond myself; I have a larger *field of intimacy* beyond myself. Within myself, everything's included.**

Intimacy always means shared identity:

- With all the split-off parts of myself
- With all the different peoples in the world
- With all the animals in the world
- With wider and wider swaths of truth, wider and wider fields of goodness, wider and wider deep understandings and experiences of beauty

My movement towards intimacy participates in the movement of evolution towards intimacy.

> *Evolution equals the evolution of intimacy.*

That's shocking. **The movement "from simplicity to complexity," which is normally understood as the evolutionary movement**—complexity means more nodes of connection—**covers up what's really happening, which is** *the progressive deepening of intimacy.*

We often use words to cover things up.

For example, someone says, "It's an amino acid. Oh, that's an amino acid reaction." What's an amino acid? Envision an amino acid in your mind, and then envision the relationship between the different parts of an amino acid—you'll see that an amino acid is actually a unique configuration of intimacy linking different, unique, discrete expressions.

Chemical expressions coming together in a particular pattern, which is a pattern of intimacy: We call that an amino acid. Then the amino acids come together in another dance or pattern of intimacy, but we just say "amino acid." We forget what it means.

**How do we understand Source, or the Tao, or God, or Geist, or the Eternal Logos?**

**That's the Infinity of Intimacy.**

The Infinity of Intimacy holds us, shares identity with us. We share identity, we're part of the Infinity of Intimacy, and at the same time, the Infinity of Intimacy literally holds us and knows our name.

Just like you hear me talking, and I hear you talking, the Field of LoveIntelligence hears us talking. No prayer is unreceived. Wow!

We're going to create a new intimacy that we've never known or offered ever before. We're going to offer our holy and broken *Hallelujah* before the divine throne.

## THE TAO THAT CAN BE SPOKEN IS NOT THE TAO

I want, with your permission, to read you something. This is from two Taoist texts, particularly from the *Tao Te Ching*. It's a gorgeous text, and it's about what the Tao is.

> *Thirty spokes are joined at the hub.*
> *From their non-being arises the function of the wheel.*
> *Lumps of clay are shaped into a vessel.*
> *From their non-being arises the function of the vessel.*
> *Doors and windows are constructed together to make a chamber.*
> *From their non-being arises the function of the chamber.*
> *Gaze at it; there's nothing to see, it's called the formless.*
> *Heed it; there's nothing to hear, it's called the soundless.*
> *Grasp it; there's nothing to hold onto, it's called the immaterial.*
> *Invisible, it cannot be called by any name.*
> *That's the authentic and profound nothingness.*
> *Contemplate the ultimate void, the Tao.*
> *Remain truly in quiescence—meaning, receiving it.*
> *All things are together in action, but I look at their non-action.*

**The Tao is that which creates the alive value of experience, that which creates and brings everything together. After it's brought together technically, functionally, it actually becomes something, and that thing has value. It has intrinsic beingness.**

That beingness comes not from technically putting it together; it comes from non-being. What the Taoists mean by non-being is the Infinity of Intimacy that is inherent in all of Cosmos.

You can't quite speak it.

The Tao that can be spoken is not the Tao.

The Tao that can be measured is not the Tao.

**The Tao that can be coded is not the Tao—but the Tao is Value itself. All Value is the Tao.**

All existence is being breathed into form every second, but not by technically putting parts together. Rather, when these parts come together, they form a whole, and that wholeness is the Tao.

So, for example, every single person on this phone call, if you sold all of the chemicals and minerals that make you up, you'd get about $7.30. You're about $7.30 worth of chemicals. If you then sold all the nerve cable that makes you up, you'd make another twenty bucks. But you are not that.

That's not your value.

**Your value is not the commodification of your various parts on the market. Your value is revealed when *all* of the different parts of you come together.**

> *That which holds you, which gives you form, is the Tao. It's the incessant, ceaseless breath of Reality.*

That's the deepest understanding of what quantum physics is pointing towards—quantum physics is not the Tao but points towards the Tao.

This *pointing towards*, it's present literally everywhere.

## THE DEATH OF OUR HUMANITY BEGINS WHEN WE THINK WE'VE STEPPED OUT OF THE TAO

The second you step out of the Tao, it's not that you become a bad human. You don't become a bad human by stepping out of the Tao. **You cease to be human.** Now, of course you can't actually ever step out of the Tao because the Tao infuses everything. So actually you don't ever step out of the Tao, but **you have the** *experience of stepping out*:

- You contract.
- Your self-understanding is alienated from your true nature.
- Your understanding of self and Reality itself is alienated from the true nature of what is, and you experience yourself as being out of the Tao.

For example, in dogmatic, materialist science, they say, "There is no Tao." You reduce everything to its "it" quality, to its physical qualities, and you forget that *physics itself is animated by the Tao*—this is why physics produces biology, and why biology produces psychology. Cosmological evolution produces biological evolution. Matter produces life. The physiosphere produces the biosphere, and the biosphere produces the noosphere, the self-reflective mind, and humanity.

**When I'm having the experience of being in the Tao, I'm living in Value.** All that's immeasurable is in the Tao, and everything we hold precious is in the Tao.

The second we step out of the Tao, it's not that we become bad humans. We simply stop being human; we no longer experience ourselves as human beings.

In the first, or second, or third generation, after we step out of the Tao, we might still be good people because we remember the old Tao; we borrow our social capital from the old Tao. But we've stepped out. Once we've stepped out, anything can happen.

Fifteen percent of the world are refugees. What do we do with the refugees? Do we really take care of them?

The second we've stepped out of the Tao, we start doing game theoretic dynamics on the value of human life… *do you begin to get where this is going?*

> ## *Much of what's happening in the world today is because we've stepped out of the Tao.*

Modernity introduced the idea of human rights, of the irreducible worth of every human being— this is one of its greatest gifts. But then modernity (and later postmodernity) stepped out of the Tao. It said, *This idea's a good idea; we believe in it, but it's a social construction. We refuse to claim it as the Evolution of Value itself.*

When you step out of the Tao, it all falls apart. So we have to step back into the Tao. Political will, a politics of evolutionary love, only can live within the Tao. And we need to articulate this language together.

That's what Outrageous Love is.

Outrageous Love emerges from the Tao; it's an expression of the Tao. To commit Outrageous Acts of Love is to articulate the *new* Tao.

**Because the Tao is not only the eternal Tao—it's also the evolving Tao.**

# CHAPTER NINE

# YOUR HOLY AND YOUR BROKEN ARE BOTH HALLELUJAH: BEING THE NEW HUMAN IN THE TAO

*Episode 230 — March 7, 2021*

## WE ARE A UNIQUE SELF SYMPHONY, AN EMERGENT EXPRESSION OF THE TAO

We are a Unique Self Symphony. A Unique Self Symphony is an expression of a new, emergent meme—a new, emergent structure of Cosmos. And we're here to tell the new story based on these new, emergent structures.

These new structures are the integration of the best interior sciences:

- The sciences of rapture
- The sciences of integrity
- The sciences of love
- The sciences of Eros
- The sciences of all that is of ultimate Value

All of these are merged with the best of the exterior sciences in all domains, brought together as those sciences appeared:

- In the traditional, premodern era
- In the modern era
- In these last decades, in this postmodern time

**We're weaving it all together, and we're articulating the new story.** We're articulating the *shared human Story of Value* within which we all live, which animates our lives and which must animate our structures of *governance*, and our structures of *politics*, and our structures of *economics*, and the *depth of our relationships*.

**Unique Self Symphony is one of those structures.**

Unique Self Symphony is an emergent expression of the Tao.

---

*The Tao, which means the intrinsic value of Cosmos, is not only eternal in the sense of unchanging; the eternal Tao is the evolving Tao.*

---

That's wildly important.

It's not just that love is eternal.

It's not just that Reality is Eros.

It's not just that loyalty, and integrity, and fairness, and goodness are values of Cosmos.

It's not just that these are expressions of the eternal Tao.

The eternal Tao is the evolving Tao, so these eternal principles—rooted in different ways in the worlds of matter, life, and mind—*all evolve*.

There are universal values intrinsic to Cosmos, but they're not preordained in the sense of being unchanging; they're also evolving. That's critical because: **the only way you can establish a sense of a shared human story is to know there's a universal grammar of value.**

And that's the single most important invitation in this time between worlds and time between stories.

## THE UNIQUE SELF SYMPHONY IN RESPONSE TO THE TECH PLEX

Unique Self Symphony means that each of us is:

- Playing our distinct role.
- Giving our Unique Gift.
- Being our unique being.
- Responding to the unique need in our unique circle of intimacy and influence, with the unique gorgeousness—the irreducible, unique expression of consciousness, desire, and intimacy—that lives in us, through us, and as us.

As such, we play our unique instrument in the Unique Self Symphony.

That's a vision, friends, not of a top-down tech plex attempting to control Reality. It's not what my brother Zak and I are calling "TechnoFeudalism." It's not a technocracy. It's not the emergence of a *Homo Deus*, a human being that can augment their reality until they become a technomorph God.

Our vision is an image of the human being who's fully human, who reaches for the sky and is yet fragile, who's noble and yet struggling.

The human being who is:

- Filled with value.
- Filled with yearning.
- Filled with goodness.
- Filled with the intuition of truth.
- Filled with the longing for beauty.

This is an image of the human being who plays their instrument, in all of its poignancy and all of its power, in the Unique Self Symphony.

**It's not a top-down model**. It's not imposed governance, either by the tech plex or by government.

**It's a bottom-up revolution.** It's the human being—me and you, us—in this Unique Self Symphony, participating as the self-actualizing Cosmos.

**It is the self-organizing Universe awakening in us. It's the evolutionary impulse moving in all of us.**

And then we pulse together in the music of Unique Self Symphony.

## IMAGINE A UNIQUE SELF FACEBOOK WITH 7.7 BILLION USERS JOINING TOGETHER IN SYMPHONY

It's not by accident that the internet is exploding and also being hijacked by the tech plex.

We need to take the internet back. **We need the internet to be not controlled by a few tech giants, but literally be the nervous system of the planet: self-organizing, creating, empowering, giving voice.** It cannot be based on the lowest common denominator aspects of human nature.

As it exists now, Facebook collects your data and sells it to third parties, creating unimaginable profits. They are defacing and abusing the nervous system of the planet: human beings are being destroyed, downgraded in a fundamental way, being manipulated and slowly erased—this is what the tech plex is doing today.

Imagine, instead, that we had a Unique Self Facebook, a social media site where everyone is sharing their Unique Self stories. It's not driven by "like" buttons and views; it's driven by genuine appreciation.

- It's driven by being willing to be madly delighted by each other.
- It's driven by authenticity.
- It's driven by vulnerability, fierceness, and tenderness.

Imagine Unique Self Facebook with 7.7 billion users joining together in symphony to address the needs of their unique circle of intimacy and influence.

## EVOLUTIONARY LOVE CODE: THE ETERNAL TAO IS THE EVOLVING TAO

There are two core existential risks. The first is the death of humanity. The second is the death of *our* humanity.

The death of our humanity begins when we think we have stepped out of the Tao. We live in the Tao. To actually step out of the Tao is impossible, but to *think* we have stepped out of the Tao is, in many ways, the greatest existential risk of all.

The Tao that can be measured is not the Tao. The Tao that can be coded is not the Tao. Words, code, and measurement can point towards the Tao.

The eternal Tao is the evolving Tao.

We can't activate a Planetary Awakening in Love through Unique Self Symphonies unless we engage from within the Tao.

There's no political will outside of the Tao.

Political will is only activated from a sense of value. When values are violated, we stand for the value. When we yearn to fulfill a value, we activate political will.

**Political will means a value needs to be fulfilled: a value has been violated, and therefore we have to activate political will.**

Remember the American Revolution, the French Revolution when the Bastille fell, or other national struggles, such as the Dutch fight for freedom.

Let's take the American Revolution as an example: The Americans grew cotton and then the law was to sell that cotton to a monopoly, which was the British West India Company. The British West India Company would buy that cotton, spin it into cloth, and then sell that cotton back to the colonists.

The colonists said:

This is a violation of value. It's not an economic value issue. That's an expression of it, but why should the goods created by us be forced to be sold to you, moved across the ocean, then made into cloth, and then sold back to us at an astronomical profit? That doesn't make sense. That's a violation of our relationship to the means of production. That's a violation of fairness. That's a violation of goodness. There's something untrue about it; it's not beautiful.

That was the basis of the American Revolution.

In France, the Bastille fell because there was a similar realization of the values of liberty, equality, and fraternity.

> *Political will is only activated when we're in the Tao, when we're in Value— and Value also lives in us.*

**Value is not a social construction of Reality.** It's not a fiction. It's not an imagined construct, as our postmodern friends like to claim. **No, value is real. Value also evolves. Value is in the Tao. The Tao is eternal, but eternal doesn't mean unchanging. Eternal means** *that which is beneath time, and that which is beneath place.* **The eternal is the timeless time and the placeless place.**

The eternal Tao doesn't mean the Tao never changes. The Tao is rooted in eternal structures that are evolving.

### LOVE IS BOTH ETERNAL AND IT EVOLVES

Outrageous Love is the love that moves the sun and other stars.

It's the love that's the heart of existence itself.

It's Evolutionary Love, the love that drives evolution. It's the love that motivates the evolution of love itself. That love evolves. It looks different today—love feels and is activated in very different ways today than it was 2,000 years ago.

Love evolves, and we participate in its evolution, but it's always love. It's the same quality of holding, and caring, and nurturing, and ecstasy, and self-evident goodness, and self-evident truth, and self-evident beauty. **The way it manifests evolves, but love is eternal.**

**Love is evolving, and love is eternal at the same time.**

That's not some minor detail. It's these understandings that will allow us to integrate all the thought in the world and create, for the first time in history, a shared framework of value, a shared, intrinsic grammar of value that's not a social construction. This directly answers the major challenges to value that come from modernity and postmodernity.

We've articulated a notion of value that can be the ground of the new story, the ground of a global ethos for a global civilization.

Outrageous Love is an eternal value which is also an evolving value, a First Principle and First Value of Cosmos, a shared ground for the new story. It is the scaffolding of a global ethos for a global civilization that will allow us to activate global coherence, to overcome the global intimacy disorder, and to move towards a Planetary Awakening in Love Through Unique Self Symphonies.

We're saying this as the revolutionaries we are together. It's our job to speak, to make our declarations. But not because *we made it up*, and not because *it's a conjecture*, but because this new story comes **from the deepest respect, devotion, studies, scholarship, ecstasy, and Eros.**

## THE TAO IS THE REALIZATION OF THE UNQUANTIFIABLE VALUE OF A HUMAN BEING

We can't make quantified, algorithmic, tech plex, game theoretic moves because each person's value is immeasurable and irreducible. That's the

Tao. **The Tao is the realization that my own individuated value, my instrument in the Unique Self Symphony, has immeasurable worth, irreducible value, and infinite quality: it's irreducible, indestructible, and eternal.**

That's the nature of value. That is what it means to be in the Tao. **It means that the personhood of the human being is not quantifiable, and that personhood is priceless beyond all measure.** That only makes sense in the Tao.

That's not the individual as a construct developed by nineteenth-century political philosophy. Nor is it a twentieth-century existentialist expression about the importance of the first-person voice, as it's often stated. Sartre was the apostle for cosmic meaninglessness, and although he talks about the beauty of the first-person voice, he's basically saying, *That's just our assertion in the face of a meaningless Cosmos, and it's also meaningless.*

That's not what the Tao is saying.

**That ecstatic urgency to assert my first-person voice and then to have it—not isolated, or alienated, or dissociated or narcissistic, but— recognized as a unique instrument in the Unique Self Symphony: that's the Tao.**

That's my intrinsic nature.

It's intrinsically valuable and precious beyond all measure.

**The Tao is all the different ways that we experience this sense of immeasurable, irreducible value.**

## THERE'S A SHATTERING IN EVERYTHING THAT REALITY HAS MADE—THAT'S HOW THE LIGHT GETS IN

There's a very beautiful text which speaks of a story from one of the great, ancient, mystical, mythic texts in world history. It's the story of *Moshe*,

Moses, who ascends Mount Sinai, one of the great mystical images of Western culture.

When he ascends the mountain, the finite goes to meet the Infinite; the human voice goes to hear the divine voice. **Prophecy and prayer meet. The human and God, the Infinite and the finite, the All-Powerful and the all-poignant, come together.**

In the mystical image, Moses receives these tablets of wisdom, these tablets of the Tao, these tablets of law, these tablets of love, *Luchot HaBrit*, the Tablets of the Covenant that are meant to go in the Ark of the Covenant. Recall Indiana Jones in *Raiders of the Lost Ark*, that movie from forty years ago, where we see the Ark of the Covenant that lived in the Tabernacle in the desert and later in Solomon's Temple in Jerusalem.

Moses comes down the mountain and sees that the people who had just been ecstatically open, who had just seen visions of Love and Spirit unlike any that had ever been seen in human history, these same people were now filled with fear because Moses hadn't yet descended from the mountain. They have turned and fallen, and been somehow degraded, and some had been led astray. The mystical symbol for this being led astray, for this degradation, is the golden calf, meaning somehow losing their way, losing their direction.

So then Moses shatters the tablets.

Then, in a fierce contestation with infinite Source, with the Divine, Moses demands that he be allowed to ascend the mountain again so that the people have a second chance—because everyone gets a second chance, and everyone gets a third chance, and everyone gets a fourth chance. It's never over. He demands from the Divine a second set of tablets. The first set of tablets are broken, and Moses receives a second set of whole tablets to put in the Ark of the Covenant.

Then he hears a whisper of the divine voice. The third-century mystics, in Aramaic and in Hebrew, tell us what that divine whisper was. I'll say it to you, with your permission, in the original language. The mystics say, *Luchot ve'shivrei luchot mu'nachim ba'aron*: "The tablets and the broken tablets are both in the Ark of the Covenant." Wow.

Then the people fell.

- They fell into depression.
- They fell into bipolar episodes.
- They fell into a devastation.
- They fell into contraction.
- They fell into an inability to feel their own beauty, their own goodness, their own truth.
- They fell into jealousy.
- They fell into rage.
- They fell into all sorts of acting out.

They fell, they broke. *And yet*, the text says, *even that is holy*. Not just that the whole tablets are in the Ark, but *Luchot ve'shivrei luchot mu'nachim ba'aron*, "The whole tablets *and* the broken tablets are both in the Ark."

Leonard Cohen received this lineage tradition, and out of it he wrote the song, "Hallelujah," which includes both the holy and the broken.

*It doesn't matter what you heard. There's a blaze of light in every word. The holy and the broken Hallelujah.* That's where it's from.

What do we tend to think is in the Ark?

- We think that it's only the good moments.
- We think it's when we're pretty.
- We think it's when we're writing a great book.
- We think it's when we're showing up really well and everyone is dazzled by our goodness, and by our strength, and by our wisdom, and our beauty.

No, that's not true, my friends.

# IN THE TAO

I was talking to someone the other day who was in the midst of a deep, broken moment. I said to this person, who's a dear person in my life:

It doesn't matter to me whether you're calling me because your book just hit the *New York Times* bestseller list and you're getting accolades from all over the world and everyone loves you, and I'm giving you a big congratulations—or you're in the state that you're now in, which is you're in your broken *Hallelujah*.

You're going to get from me the same dignity, the same love, and the same knowing that you're gorgeous, that you're holy, and that you're broken—*Hallelujah*. I treat you with enormous dignity, honor, and love.

They're both in the Ark of the Covenant.

So I want to invite us now to feel deeply into the holy and broken *Hallelujah*. This is the first way to know you're in the Tao.

The second way of knowing you're in the Tao is knowing that your suffering is not an accident, that there's no suffering that's accidental, there are no tears that are lost. **Every tear is drunk and swallowed by the Infinity of Intimacy.**

The holy and the broken *Hallelujah*.

- Nothing escapes.
- Nothing is extra.
- Nothing is frivolous.
- Every place you've been, you needed to be.
- Every tragedy is not some bug in the system; it's a feature.
- Every fall is part of the next rise.
- Every destruction creates the next creation.
- Every breaking opens us up.

Can you feel it?

**There's a crack, there's a shattering in everything that Reality has made, and that's how the light gets in.**

To know you're in the Tao is to know:

- No tear is shed in vain.
- No brokenness is lost; it's all held in dignity, it's all part of the Story; we don't rip out pages from our book of life.
- We love each other even more madly open when we're broken.

To be in the Tao is to know that the world is filled with broken hearts, and broken vessels, and broken stories, and broken bodies… **but there's nothing more whole than a broken heart.**

We can also touch the Tao in knowing and feeling each other's irreducible value: *you're priceless, I can't sell you no matter what it will bring*—and the algorithmic, game theoretic dynamic falls away.

### RESHIMU: TRACES OF TRANSCENDENCE

The Tao also shows up in what I want to call "traces of transcendence." Imagine this. Say you have a porcelain jug from which you drink, and that jug has wine in it. It's filled with wine. So you empty the wine out, and then you thoroughly wash the jug. Then you put water in that jug, and you taste the water.

So, friends, when you taste the water, what else do you taste? You taste traces of the wine.

Those traces of wine are called by the lineage masters, *reshimu*. They're "traces," they're "impressions" of the wine.

- You can't see the wine.
- You can't even speak the wine.
- You can't code the wine.
- You can't measure the wine

The Tao that can be measured is not the Tao, and the Tao that can be coded is not the Tao, and the Tao that can be spoken is not the Tao—and yet the wine is there, clear and unmistakable. And it changes your whole experience.

1. The first place that we experience traces of transcendence is in knowing your irreducible value, knowing my irreducible value, knowing *I'm not going to be sold* and *I'm not going to be sold out*, that there's an intrinsic loyalty to me in Cosmos. *Wow!* That's shocking.

*I can't be betrayed.*

*I can't be sold down the river.*

*I can't be sold out.*

*I can't be sold.*

*I have irreducible value.*

2. *My suffering is never in vain. My tears are never lost, never.* That's the second experience, *when I realize the dignity of my suffering.*

It doesn't mean I need to wallow in my suffering.

I often say to my friends, who have asked me about suffering in my personal life, "At a certain point, I got bored with my own suffering." We can let go of our own suffering. But that's only when we're ready to let go of it, and no one can tell us to let go of it.

We have to hold the dignity of each other's pain, which is what the sacred text says. *Bekol tza'aro'tam, lo tza'ar,* "In all of your suffering, She suffers with you." That's the second arena of the Tao.

3. The third arena of the Tao is in the sacredness of play.

Have you ever watched children play, when they enter into a game and they make up new rules? They enter into play with enormous delight, enormous gravitas, and enormous seriousness. **When I enter into play, I realize traces of eternity.** It's why we watch sports events. So many sports events, though, have sadly been commodified, reduced, and marketed.

**At the core, at the center of play—play between children, play between adults—is the whisper of eternity.** Whether it's our love sport or our love play, whether it's athletic play, whether it's the play of laughter—**in the laughter, in the sport, and in the play is the echo of eternity.**

We feel the goodness of it all; we feel how it all matters beyond imagination— which is why sometimes **it's when we play together that we're able to evolve the source code of consciousness and culture.**

I'd like to have an institute in which we bring all the world leaders together— and that's all of us—to play together:

- Let's play in sports.
- Let's play in love.
- Let's play with our minds.
- Let's play with laughter.

And from that place of play, *let's evolve consciousness.*

There's a beautiful TV series called *The English Game*, which is about football in England in the mid-nineteenth century, when it was originally an upper-class sport of the landed gentry. Then the textile mills start a football team, and a friendship is struck between a working-class player and a player from the upper class. In that friendship and in their play, in their respect for the dignity of play and their realization of their core equality in play, there's this deep social evolution that takes place and opens up a next stage in the evolution of love. *The English Game,* it's beautiful. So, let's play.

    4.   Finally, friends, we find traces of transcendence in music; when we chant, when we sing.

Music itself is the language of intimacy. Music itself is a trace of transcendence.

We've just listed four traces of transcendence:

1. My own experience of irreducible value, both mine and yours.
2. The experience that I never suffer alone, that my suffering is meaningful and not random. The dignity, even the holiness, of my holy and broken *Hallelujahs*. All my broken Hallelujahs are also holy. *There's a blaze of light in every word. It doesn't matter what you heard. It's the holy and the broken Hallelujah.* That's the Tao. That's a trace of transcendence.
3. The sacredness of play.
4. The disclosed Intimate Universe that appears in the chords of music that move through us and transform us.

These are rumors of angels. These are traces of transcendence. **These are the Tao that cannot be spoken, but which is all around us, and which suffuses us. Political will that's genuine comes from an alignment with value. And all value lives in the Tao.**

1. The value of irreducible uniqueness.
2. The value of our holy and broken Hallelujah.
3. The intrinsic value of our play.
4. The gorgeous value of our music.

These are but four traces of transcendence.

But look all around and drink: drink from the jugs, drink from the urns, drink from the flasks, and feel all the traces.

They're always there.

# CHAPTER TEN

# EVOLUTION IS PERSONAL: A SCIENTIFIC TRUTH

*Episode 231 — March 14, 2021*

### WE ARE EVOLUTION IN PERSON

We are here to participate in the evolution of love. But to participate in the evolution of love, we need to know that Reality's not merely a fact—Reality's a story. There's a narrative arc to Cosmos. We mean that not figuratively, and not merely metaphorically, and not merely symbolically. **There's a literal narrative arc to Cosmos.**

Cosmos has so far moved through three Big Bangs. The First Big Bang was the emergence of Reality itself as we know it. The Second Big Bang was the radical, momentous leap to life. The Third Big Bang occurred when life itself took a momentous leap of both continuity and discontinuity, and the depths of the self-reflective human mind emerged.

There's a narrative arc to Cosmos: stage after stage, level after level. **Each level differentiates from the previous level and brings something into being that's radically novel and radically new, including the best, the deepest, of everything that came before.**

Human beings have within them all of matter, all of life, and all of mind. The memory of Cosmos lives in us. Cosmos lives in us.

Human science works because we're cosmic humans. All of mathematics lives in us, which explains the uncanny, improbable, and impossible accuracy of mathematics—and why we're attuned to those mathematics. They flow through us. That's exterior science.

But it's not only the mathematics of structural connection but, my friends, also the mathematics of intimacy. Not just exterior science but interior science lives in us. And interior science works, again, because we are cosmic humans; **we participate in the interior face of Cosmos.** And so we can stand here and say **we are evolution in person.**

We're aligning with the evolutionary impulse that beats uniquely in us personally.

We come together as Unique Selves, unique expressions of the Evolutionary Impulse—we're not just the results of a Myers-Briggs test or a personality type. **I am the unique expression of the pulsing of evolution itself that lives in me, as me, and through me.**

The unique pulsing of my desire.

---

*Political will is only activated when we're in the Tao, when we're in Value— and Value also lives in us.*

---

We're going to talk about Outrageous Love. Friends, ordinary love is a strategy of the ego limited to the human realm and to particular expressions in the human realm. We limit love by exiling it to a particular romantic moment. No. That's just but one expression of the deeper movement of Cosmos itself: Outrageous Love, Eros, the Tao that drives all of Reality, that infuses everything.

The difference between ordinary love and Outrageous Love is the difference between a very high number and infinity.

## RE-READING NEUROCHEMISTRY AS AN EXPRESSION OF THE INTIMATE UNIVERSE

Deeper than the immediate risk of Covid and its new strains is the catastrophic and existential risk that's rooted in what we call a "global intimacy disorder." **The only way to overcome the global intimacy disorder is to realize that we live, quite literally, in an Intimate Universe.** That's the new Evolutionary Story. The Universe is the Story of Evolution, and Evolution is the Love Story of the Universe.

I was reading over the weekend about experiments that were done by this very important thinker, Mike Merzenich, on neuroplasticity. Neuroplasticity means the movement of the brain that is able to "re-track" itself. We thought that the brain was fixed; for many years, all the Nobel Prize winners said the brain was a fixed structure. We now know that's not true. We now know that if a particular part or a particular track in the brain is lost, the brain will retrack, or "rewire," and essentially self-correct—meaning *the brain is always changing, it's always moving, it's always shifting*.

It's very easy to misunderstand the full depth of that.

The cells in our brain are called neurons. Our neurons are not like the other cells. The neurons have a central core, which carry out their functions common to all cells, but they also have two tentacle-like appendages called axons and dendrites. An axon transmits electrical pulses to other neurons, and the dendrites receive the electrical pulses.

Freud did anatomical research before he went into psychology, and he began to get a sense of this. Everyone thought he was wrong; pretty much everyone thought the brain was a closed system. No one understood its centrality because you don't actually feel the brain beating like you feel the heart beating. You don't feel the brain like you feel the stomach. We've only recently realized, in the last 100 years, that the brain has 100 billion neurons, which are these unique, distinct cells. So listen to the sentence from Merzenich:

When a neuron is active, a pulse flows from the soma, which is the center of the cell, to the tip of the axon, where it triggers the release of chemicals called neurotransmitters. The neurotransmitters flow across the contact barrier, the synapse, and attach themselves to a dendrite of a neighboring neuron, triggering or suppressing a new electrical pulse in that cell. It's through the flow of neurotransmitters across synapses that neurons communicate with one another, directing the transmission of electrical signals along complex cellular pathways. Thoughts, memories, and emotions all emerge from the electrochemical interactions of the neurons mediated by synapses.

This is very wild. You could completely miss the Universe: A Love Story in these sentences. It sounds like we're just talking about electrical signals that pulse through the brain—but what is an electrical signal? An electrical signal is a configuration of electrons. And it's a configuration of electrons in unique patterns of *allurement*; that's what an electrical signal is. Now, what the neurons are doing in a cell is editing its own DNA code. The cellular structure is rewriting its own DNA code. A cellular structure is a unique structure of allurement with unique relationships between the different parts of the cell. It's an utterly unique pattern.

The cell is semi-autonomous. The cell is intelligent, literally writing, rewriting, and editing its own DNA. These neurons transmit electrical signals, which are unique configurations of allurement, unique patterns of intimacy, which we're calling electrical pulses. Those unique patterns of intimacy, those electrical pulses, trigger the release of neurotransmitters, but what's a neurotransmitter? That's just a word. The word's in the way.

A neurotransmitter means a particular set of chemicals. And what's a chemical? **A chemical is a unique configuration of intimately allured and configured particles that are arranged.** Have you ever seen a picture of a chemical? It's a unique arrangement of intimacy, and a set of chemicals is a unique arrangement of intimacies organized into a larger intimate symphony. So the pulse of uniquely configured allurement of electrons, in a unique pattern of intimacy, moves across through the axons. The axons are, as it were, the phallus of the neuron. That phallus is received by the dendrites, the yoni of the next neuron. There's a pulsing, a throbbing of this unique pattern of allurement, which then activates, if you will, the wetness, the semen, the tumescence of the cell: the neurotransmitters that are thrust through. Wow!

In other words, what's happening between these neurons is unique configurations and patterns of allurement. What drives the cell all the time is this allurement to allurement, this drive towards intimacy that's living and uniquely configured in the cell. The cell has axons, its phallic thrust; dendrites are receiving, pulsing, and throbbing. That pulsing pattern and throbbing activates chemicals. **Those chemicals are themselves unique patterns of allurement.**

You can read the sentence again and think only of neurotransmitters, dendrites, axons, neurons, and cells. You'd have no idea what you're talking about. You're just using a word to obfuscate, to occlude, to cloud what's happening at the core of Reality. Reality is kissing all the time. Reality is in a constant state of unique configurations of allurement. This is not just general or generic allurement. These are unique configurations of allurement. It's pretty hot up there; it's pretty hot everywhere. That's wild. You can read the sentence and realize that you're completely alienated from the intimacy that throbs and pulses at the heart of Cosmos. **You may not realize that the same drive to intimacy that pulses in you, in me, in we, in thee, in She—pulses all the way up and all the way down Reality.**

Reality is a Field of Intimacy, and Reality is sourced in the Infinity of Intimacy.

When we say the difference between ordinary love and Outrageous Love is the difference between a very high number and infinity, what we're saying is that, scientifically—in both the exterior and interior sciences—**Reality is sourced in the Infinity of Intimacy, and Reality is a Field of Intimacies.**

Now, that's not Pollyannish. That's actually the nature of Reality.

And the only way we can ever talk about evil is that because it's an Intimate Universe, evil is a failure of intimacy. Alienation is a failure of intimacy. Depersonalization is a failure of intimacy.

And again, intimacy is not just generic; intimacy is absolutely, radically personal. Those 100 billion neurons in your brain are uniquely individuated expressions of the Infinity of Intimacy signed as your name. That's the truth of Reality.

## IN PRAYER WE TURN TO THE INFINITY OF INTIMACY THAT KNOWS OUR NAME

So in this moment, friends, we're going to pray, which means we're going to turn to the Infinity of Intimacy that knows our name.

Some people call that the Tao, and other people call it Eros, and some people call it God, and other people call it Mut, and other people call it Geist, and other people call it the Eternal Logos, and other people call it *Adonai Eloheinu*, and other people call it Atman is Brahman, and other people call it *sunyata*. These are all different qualities, different experiences of the same Infinity of Intimacy.

And that Infinity of Intimacy is not just third person. It's not just an "It," some flowing, impersonal generic force. That is one important quality of Cosmos, and it's a First Principle of Cosmos. But there's also the second person, the personhood of Cosmos that knows my name. Reality is screaming: *I know your name.*

It's the She that sits in a chair next to me and loves me madly. It's all of the third person—all of the God in the third person, all of the love in the third person, all the Eros in the third person—sitting in a chair, looking at me, knowing me, caring desperately about me. It's the personhood of protons all the way up and all the way down. It's the Infinity of Intimacy that knows my name. That's the second person, and that's a First Principle and First Value of Cosmos. Finally, that experience of second person lives in me personally, so I have a mad desire to love you and to know you, and you have a mad desire to love me and know me—not just in the narrow confines of "one person's romantic love." Outrageous Love.

We're a band of Outrageous Lovers. Loving each other doesn't mean we get a U-Haul, get married, and live together. For some of us, it may mean that, but that's one instantiation of the beautiful and Amorous Cosmos.

But it means we actually get to love each other.

We get to be excited about each other.

We get to marry each other again and again and again in *hieros gamos*, the marriage of two parts that become a larger whole. Then we come together, Unique Selves in a Unique Self Symphony, and we become the unique expressions of the self-actualizing Cosmos, the self-organizing Universe, acting for healing and transformation, acting to feed every hungry child, acting to hold every broken heart. *Wow!*

We can't do it alone, friends. We can never do it alone. We turn to God. Not the cosmic vending-machine god—the god you don't believe in doesn't exist—but the Infinity of Intimacy that knows our name, **and we ask for everything**. We ask for everything because prayer affirms the dignity of personal need. And if my personal need is not dignified, how can I act as a unique, intimate partner of the Infinity of Intimacy? So we're going to pray now with Leonard Cohen, who's with us every week. This hymn affirms the truth of the Tao, which is that *nothing's left out*.

*Nothing is extra*. Everything is included, our holy and our broken *Hallelujah*.

*There's a blaze of light in every word.*

We turn and we pray to the Infinity of Intimacy, and we ask for literally everything.

We wrap these prayers and bind to these roses, and we lift them, literally, like a prayer to the sky. Amen. Let's find each other, friends, all the way. We're going to do something here really special.

Right now, we're going to look at a sacred text, but before we read the text I want to read you the end of the code. Are we ready, friends? Let's do something we've never done before, and let's be the story. Let's be the revolution.

We are da Vinci. We are standing in this time between worlds and this time between stories.

We're telling the new story, and we're articulating new Evolutionary Love codes every week.

We're going to articulate a new dimension of this code right now.

The Tao that can be measured is not the Tao.

The Tao that can be coded is not the Tao.

The Tao is pointed towards by words, by code, by measurement, but it's deeper than that.

It's immeasurable. It's priceless. It's beyond.

> *The Tao, friends, is Value. It's the intrinsic Value that lives in Cosmos underneath everything.*

## THE INTERNET IS THE SHALLOWS, THE CLARIFIED HEART-MIND EXPRESSES DEPTH

There's a book about the internet by Nicholas Carr called "The Shallows." And "shallow" is the opposite of "deep." In interior science, what we call the Holy of Holies, or the Inside of the Inside, is also called *umka d'umka*, which is "the deepest of the deep," "the depths of the depth." The opposite of the holy is not the unholy; the opposite of the holy is the superficial.

**Omek** is "depth." Depth is the Tao, the Infinite Depth.

The "shallow," the surface, or the superficial is called *gavan* in the lineage. **The opposite of the sacred, the opposite of the holy, is the superficial.**

Now, what is the internet? The internet is *the shallows*, which means that there's no time or place for depth. It's why Mike Merzenich, who did this fantastic research on brain neuroplasticity, talks about the "negative neuroplasticity" generated by the structure of the internet, which he calls "the shallows." Carr borrows the name of his book from Merzenich's fantastic research—for which he won a Nobel Prize for—showing that **the incarnate structure of the online experience is about complete interruption, inability to focus, inability to concentrate, the stealing and hijacking of attention.** However:

> *It's attention that blooms our ability to access the interior of Reality. So why have we generated an internet that is "the shallows?"*

Here's the story, and it's very painful.

And we've got to realize it's very powerful—because **we have to recode the internet with Evolutionary Love.**

The internet is an exterior expression of us having stepped out of the Tao. When we step out of the Tao, when we step out of Value, when we step out of the realization:

- That Reality is interior all the way up and all the way down.
- That exteriors are parallel with this full interior world of infinite depth.
- That the interior face of the Cosmos is absolutely and utterly real.

*If I don't realize that, then there's no reason to concentrate.*

There's no reason to focus.

There's no reason to sit silently in the depth of reading a book.

*I'm just going to scroll and click and descend into the bottomless pit of recurring advertisements and be translated into and affected and moved around by algorithms that are constantly stealing my attention.*

*Then I realize that I'm exhausted.*

> **We're literally losing our ability to do that which is most human: to be sapiens, to be thoughtful, to plumb the interior depth of the Cosmos.**

To do that:

- I have to rest.
- I have to go inside.
- I have to access Outrageous Love.
- I have to access the ecstatic urgency pulsing through Cosmos.
- I have to access the deep silence of contemplation.
- I have to enter into Value.

That's depth.

The opposite of depth is "the shallows." And the internet is the exterior expression of the postmodern mind—which uncoincidentally arose at the same time as the internet—that says, *we're going to deconstruct all Value.*

"Everything is a mere fiction," writes Yuval Harari—Chapter Two in *Sapiens*. "It's a mere imagined reality, and imagination is just a social construction of reality."

If that's true, then why go slow? Then why go deep? There's no reason to go deep because there is no ultimate depth.

Depth means *the Tao*.

Depth means *it's not a fiction*.

Depth means *it's not contrived*.

Depth means *it's not merely a social construction,*

Rather:

---

*That which the social body and its clarified heart-mind construct is actually an expression of the Tao.*

---

So now let's take it one step further. We're going to read a sacred text. Because the evolutionary impulse has to be informed by sacred text. This is a text from one of the great mystics, one of the great interior scientists of the twentieth century, Abraham Kook. Here's what he writes:

It sometimes happens that the person falls into smallness and cannot find within herself any inner contentment because of the non-impact of her good deeds.

In other words, *My life doesn't quite add up*. In other words, *I had a dream about my life*:

- I thought love was going to look a certain way, and I thought it was going to taste a certain way.
- I thought I was going to live in a particular context.
- I thought I was going to feel a certain way.

*But somehow my good deeds, my choices, didn't add up to the life that I dreamed.*

How many people recognize the possibility *that all my intentions and all my actions didn't add up to the life I thought I was going to live?*

And then *I fall into smallness* because of the calculated sum of my misses.

I feel like I missed. But that's a mistake.

Kook writes: *This person must strengthen himself with the mystery power of thought. This person must enter into the Palace of Thought.*

What's the "Palace of Thought?"

In the Palace of Thought, *I know that there's another story that I'm living, and that's the story that I live in my heart, mind, and body.*

It's not the public story.

It's not the political story.

It's not the story of *near misses*.

It's not the story that I'm living every day, which is beautiful. I've got to embrace that story and live the story in the best possible way—but actually that's not the only place I live. That's one gorgeous, important place.

There's a second place I live, and that's in the Palace of Thought.

You have to know that your thought is more valued by She, than all impactful, fulfilled actions.

Know that the Palace of Thought is absolutely real. It's more real than real.

We think that Reality is what appears on the outside. That's just one expression of Reality.

**The Palace of Thought, the Palace of Imagination, is more real to the Holy One, more blessed be She, than all our supposedly impactful actions.** Since this is so: holy thought, exalted images of the imagination, as well as scenes of beauty, love, desire, and fulfillment, all possess the same Reality as the impactful actions.

That's what it means to be in the Tao.

- It's not based on *did it turn out okay?*

- It's not based on *did the story have the ending I thought it should have?*
- It's not based on *did it turn out the way I wanted it to turn out?*
- **I know that I live in the Palace of Imagination, in the Palace of Thought, and that the Palace is real.**

Again, Kook: *You should encourage yourself greatly with the fact that sometimes the paucity of actual deeds and study*—meaning the reason that my deeds haven't landed the way that I thought they would—*is because you have a strong inclination towards the secret of thought.*

In other words, you forgot that there's magic in your imagination.

There's magic in your reality-making, in your Palace of Thought.

Now stay with me, this is so beautiful, let's read the text from the inside:

*It could be that many aspects of her fallings happen*—the reason we fall in this world, a lot of the reason it doesn't manifest in this world, is—*because she did not value enough the essence of her thinking.*

She thought that it wasn't real.

She thought that Outrageous Love wasn't real.

She thought that the Palace of Thought was just imagination.

No, imagination's the most real Reality. The Palace of Thought is utterly real.

When the story of my life that I live in is one where the Palace of Thought is sacred—then I can manifest, then I can create.

*Therefore, let her strengthen herself even more with inner insight in order to understand that the fixing of the entire world and the cure, the healing for all souls, all depend on the fundamental principle of the Palace of Thought. From that place, let her raise her thought and imagination as far as she can, and she will rise to transform, from inner love.* This is Kook's phrase for what we mean by Outrageous Love.

Oh my God. Can you feel that? *Wow!*

The Palace of Thought is real. That's the Tao.

The Tao that can be manifested is not the Tao.

The Tao that can be coded is not the Tao.

The Tao that can be measured is not the Tao.

**The Tao lives in the Palace of Thought. It's the truth of the story that I fill myself with in full joy—every moment and every day.**

# CHAPTER ELEVEN

# THE ARC OF THE INTIMATE UNIVERSE BENDS TOWARD EVOLUTIONARY UNIQUE SELF

*Episode 232 — March 21, 2021*

## REALITY MOVES TOWARDS MORE INTIMACY, WHOLENESS, ALIVENESS, DEPTH, ECSTASY, AND KINDNESS

The Universe feels, and the Universe feels love. The Universe doesn't feel ordinary love; the universe feels Outrageous Love. And Outrageous Love is the ecstasy of Cosmos, the Field of Cosmos pulsing towards more intimacy, towards more wholeness.

The only reason that we're aware of evil, and why it's not considered ordinary, is because *evil is the opposite of love. And love is life.* Life is the lifeforce, the Eros of the Cosmos, which:

- Moves towards wholeness.
- Moves towards more kindness.
- Moves towards more mutuality, union, recognition, and embrace.

**Evil is a violation of that fundamental drive toward intimacy, which is why we notice it; otherwise, it would be ordinary.**

We're not just driven to survive. That's a word that evolutionary psychology uses, but it obfuscates what's actually happening. Evolutionary psychology often uses it as a way to disguise its hidden dogmatic materialist assumptions. Evolutionary psychology is only now just finally moving beyond this.

Actually, we're not moved to survive. We're moved to live. We've moved towards life. Reality is a movement towards ever more aliveness, and ever greater depth, and ever more ecstasy, and ever deeper kindness.

The movement toward that transformation takes place within us. We're moved to transform. We're moved to transform ourselves and to transform the collective and then the Cosmos. **We know that *our transformation transforms the whole thing.***

## THE PRINCIPLES OF REVOLUTION: TELLING THE NEW STORY

These principles that we're sharing right now are the principles of the revolution. These are First Principles and First Values. We live in this time between stories and this time between worlds in which we've lost our bearings. We have to regain our bearings, but in an evolutionary way.

And so we have to do precisely what our colleague—our beloved, fellow Outrageous Lover, Leonardo da Vinci—did with his cohort of a few hundred people in the Renaissance when they realized that they were at a time between worlds and a time between stories, when they were ravaged by pandemic. They said, *We're going to speak into Reality. We're going to stand at the abyss of darkness and say, "Let there be light"*—and light means an evolution of consciousness and culture.

They moved out of premodernity—in the Renaissance—and into the modern world and established new principles of Reality, which became the basis of modernity. **To the precise extent that those principles**—principles about self, narratives of self, narratives of community, narratives of a universe story, narratives of power, narratives of desire—**were**

**accurate, beautiful, good, and true, they burst into the great dignities of modernity:**

- The end of slavery.
- The emergence of the feminine.
- The gorgeousness of the scientific method.
- The full explosion of life where the average human life went from thirty years to seventy. It was also an explosion of life in terms of numbers: new human beings, new Unique Selves. We went from half a billion people 200 years ago to close to eight billion people now.
- An explosion of life: an incredible explosion of the length of life, depth of life, available choices in life, and greater mobility in life.

All of this was based on a new story.

Yet there were parts of that new story that were inaccurate.

There were parts of the narrative that were flawed and based on erroneous assumptions—and what later became false dogmas that hardened into fundamentalism—claiming that Reality was only materialist, that Reality was actually out of the Tao, that Reality didn't live in intrinsic Value.

**This great and necessary rebellion against the excesses of the great religions, against the shadows of the great religions, unfortunately turned us away from Spirit and towards a reductionist, materialist universe.**

Even in the religious world, there's the sense of, *Is it really true?*

Even in the spiritual world, they're asking, *Is it just a social construction?*

No, it's not all a social construction.

> *Love is real, Eros is real, Spirit is real—and they're the same. Spirit lives in each of us uniquely, and our stories are utterly unique, chapter and verse, in the CosmoErotic Universe, in the Intimate Universe, in what we call the Amorous Cosmos.*

We can feel the joy of it all, and we can feel the suffering of it all. We now understand that we're poised between utopia and dystopia, and **we have to tell the new story**.

That's the overriding ecstatic, moral, erotic, ethical imperative of this moment in time. And we're going to give it everything we've got.

## ALL OF REALITY IS INTIMATE, ALL THE WAY UP AND ALL THE WAY DOWN

We can feel, in this second, the *Amor*, the Outrageous Love that moves through Reality—not as a conjecture, but as the most accurate description based on the deepest interior and exterior sciences.

*Amor: Its insides are lined with love.*

That's how Solomon spoke of it. We've come from the *Song of Solomon* to contemporary physics, which is a new *Song of Solomon*; and to macromolecular understandings in molecular biology, which is a new *Song of Solomon*; and to an understanding of the neuroplastic brain and the mind as deeply intermeshed, which is a new *Song of Solomon*.

Exterior science is but a new text of the great *Song of Solomon*, and at the core it's just one word: *Amor*. In Solomon's words, *its insides are lined with love*. Let's take this into prayer.

What do we mean by prayer? We're not praying to a cosmic vending machine. Instead, we have the actual experience that *Reality is an Intimate Universe*. Let's feel it together. *Reality is relationship.*

- We're all interconnected—and we're all individuated.
- We can feel each other.
- We love each other.

Because that's the true nature of Reality. No one is a stranger. Every person is always already someone I'm in love with. It doesn't mean we're going to move in together. It means **I'm madly in love with you because we're part of the same Field of LoveDesire.**

That is the very nature of Cosmos, from subatomic particles coming together as atoms—protons, neutrons, and electrons are allured to each other, coming together synergistically in a new whole greater than the sum of the parts.

That is the same Eros that moves in me, and in thee, and he and she, and in the royal we.

That is the nature of the evolutionary chain all the way up and all the way down.

That is the nature of the Intimate Universe.

That is the nature of all of the molecular compounds.

- What's a molecule? It's a series of relationships between smaller elements (atoms) that are allured to each other and create particular configurations of intimacy that produce a more complex form.
- What's a protein? A protein is a complex structure of dazzling, configured intimacy—amino acids arranged in a particular relationship.
- What's an amino acid? An amino acid is a configuration of particular chemicals, which themselves are constructions

and configurations of intimacy.

All of Reality is intimate, all the way up and all the way down. And Reality itself is driven by the desire for ever greater intimacy. Reality is the progressive deepening of intimacies. It's not an evolution from simplicity to complexity; that's just the exterior dimension of it. It's not systems theory, meaning only interconnected exterior systems.

**It's actually interiors and exteriors interconnected and interlocked with each other.**

- It's interconnected depth.
- It's interconnected essence.

The world is not materialist and is not dualist. Jaron Lanier writes in one of his books *we might have to accept a dualistic world*. Jaron is a writer for the tech plex, and he's a good man, but he's not right about dualism. *You've got to update, my friend. It's all about pan-interiority.*

All of Reality is insides *and* outsides, all the way up and all the way down.

## THE INTERNET MUST BE RECODED FROM "THE SHALLOWS" TO DEPTH AND INTIMACY

It's about pan-depthism. It's all depth. The opposite of the holy is the superficial. That's why the internet is called "the shallows" because the internet, tragically—not in its technological structure but in the way that technology has expressed itself—is about fragmentation.

- It's about constant interruption.
- It's about the inability to drop into the inside.
- It's about monetization based on theft of data, which is then fed into machine intelligence, which is then turned into a personality profile, which is then sold to misaligned third parties who then attempt to manipulate you into doing—*not "your will," but "their will" be done*—and their will is governed

by superficial goals of power and excess and win/lose metrics.

We don't need "the shallows" of the internet, as Nicholas Carr called it, but the depths. Technology has to be coded with depth, and we need to realize we are intimate configurations of Reality.

We are God's unique intimacies. And remember: the god you don't believe in doesn't exist. God is the Infinity of Intimacy, and we are reformulating this core understanding as a revolutionary act. We turn to our Partner, who both lives in us, and breathes as us, and yet holds us at the same time. In every line in a Rumi or a Hafiz poem—or the thousands of other Sufi poets who wrote with them in that 300-year period in Kashmir and in other parts of India—every word is the realization that *we are the partner*.

**We are the friend, and we're both held by the friend at the same time.** We're held by the Infinity of Intimacy that speaks to us in second person and knows our name, even as She lives in us in first person, and we hold the wideness and depth of that truth in our ecstatic knowing. Wow.

We're going to turn now to the Infinity of Intimacy, who holds everything. And we're going to ask for everything—because that's what prayer's about— for everything *that matters*. In prayer, we discern what matters.

We affirm the dignity of our personal need. We affirm that Reality needs *us*, and we need to be in our full potency and full poignancy, in our full power, to give our Unique Gift into the depth of Reality. **We need to turn to our unique circle of intimacy and influence and be unique incarnations of divine intimacy and be the evolution of intimacy in our projects, in our posturing and our power, in all the ways that we parade our divinity.**

And She holds us.

- She holds our holy and our broken *Hallelujah*.
- She holds the whole thing.
- She holds us when we're contracted.
- She holds us when we're angry.

- She holds us when we're filled with rage.
- She holds us when we're broken.
- She holds us when we can't feel it, and She brings us home again and again.

So let's choose to go inside. Let's listen to this holy and broken *Hallelujah* of Leonard Cohen's as an ecstatic technology of finding our way into the very nature of Cosmos itself, which is infinitely intimate, held by the Infinity of Intimacy living uniquely as us as we arise together and cause a Planetary Awakening in Love through Unique Self Symphonies. The holy and the broken *Hallelujah* revolution. Take us inside, all the way.

Oh my God. Let's pray. And let's ask for everything. Prayer affirms the dignity of personal need. Let's find each other, and let's pray.

My friends, we lift all of the prayers to the sky. We offer them up, and we impress them on the lips of the divine.

Let's take this inside, and I want to take our next step in this evolution of love. So are we ready to actually do this together, the next step, full on? Nothing automatic. No automatic pilot. I've got this book I'm looking at here in front of me called *Automating Humanity*. "Everything goes into automatic."

No automatic! Ecstasy is the opposite of automatic.

- We're choosing consciously, right now, to be revolutionaries.
- We're choosing to be Outrageous Lovers.
- We're choosing to be part of the band of Outrageous Lovers, and we step in together.

Here we go.

## WHO AM I? THE SEPARATE-SELF NARRATIVE

*Who am I?* That's the greatest question that there is. It's a question that we've talked about together in so many different ways. Everything emerges from the answer to that question. And I can't answer that question without answering the questions of *where am I?* and *where do I live?*

So *who am I?* is the question of identity. At play in the world today are two fundamental narratives of identity, and we need to really understand them deeply.

The first narrative—and it appears in two forms—is a separate-self narrative. There's a religious form, and there's a materialist, secular form. They both have some truth, but they're both partial. Ultimately, they're based on fundamentally false scientific premises, both interior science and exterior science. The separate-self story says:

*I'm a separate self, and I'm obedient to God. But I'm separate from all of Reality. I was created by God, and I need to be obedient.*

Or: *I'm a separate self. I'm not part of the larger frame. I'm not part of the Field of Eros. I'm not part of the Field of Consciousness.*

That is the basic notion that underlies most democracies, for example, whether it's in a Western democracy or another system of government:

- I am in some form of a win/lose metrics.
- I'm needing to succeed in order to be valued, which means I need to produce in a way that can be commodified and sold in a particular way.
- I'm in a win/lose story governed by win/lose metrics. That is where my value comes from, and without that, I don't have intrinsic value.

That's the sense of separate self, and it's false.

## WHO AM I? THE SOCIAL-SELF NARRATIVE

The second version which is offered in Reality today—and it has a religious version and a secular version—is: *I'm a social self.* The social self might mean, in the religious version, that *I'm part of a particular religion, and my entire value comes from my standing within that particular religious—or sometimes even national religious—structure. If I'm part of that chosen people and that racial structure, I'm okay, and if I'm not, I'm not. So I'm defined by my social context entirely.*

That's one version of a social self. But then there's a more insidious version of the social self that actually dominates the internet: the social self, expressed by data science, which upgrades algorithms and downgrades human beings. It says that human beings are the sum total of their measurable actions.

We can get enough data about a human being to predict how they will act given particular stimuli. So the human being becomes a rat in a social maze: nudged and prodded by social stimuli, likes, views, all of the structures of apps, which collect data with their shiny exteriors, promising a few conveniences, but they're actually collecting massive amounts of data that are fed into machine intelligence in order to manipulate your ability to consume or vote—and ultimately influence the government and the economy.

**This is in accordance, not with your own interior value**—because you're not given enough inward space to discover that—**but in accordance with the agendas of whoever has bought the information about you** who's now using proven, split-tested methods to manipulate you. That's the social self that's illegitimate.

The social self, described by Alex Pentland in his book *Social Physics* uses mathematical formulations to figure out how to "herd" human beings, how to "tune the social herd"—Pentland's own phrases—in order to deploy long-discredited behavioral technologies introduced by B.F. Skinner to create a docile population into being the most productive it can possibly be, by eliminating "anomalies" and "exceptions," to create a kind of bland "Stepford Wives" world where everyone merely *seems* happy.

> *The social self that dominates the web is not a meta-theoretical social self—it's practical.*

In other words, the structure of surveillance capitalism, the structure of what we're calling TechnoFeudalism, gathers your data, the breadcrumbs you've left on the web. These are all exteriors:

- How long does your mouse hover before you click?
- How quickly do you click?
- What moves you to purchase?
- What order of stimuli: a picture of a cat, a five-second interval between a picture of a cat and a picture of a woman, or a four-second interval?

All this stuff is split-tested, compared to see what works best to manipulate you.

All data about you is fed into machine intelligence. But it's not merely data about you in the sense of your interior; it's data about how you react to stimuli and various forms of social pressure that goes into machine intelligence. Then, machine intelligence generates a personality profile about your exterior susceptibility, or vulnerability, to particular kinds of nudges and cues and social pressures that are beyond your pale of awareness.

That's the social self that Pentland is talking about.

> *That's the social self that we have to refuse to reduce human beings to because it's essentially the lowest common denominator of a human being.*

There are two views of human beings:

1. Let's find the observable unconscious actions of human beings, aggregate them into a social profile, define the human being by their susceptibility to be manipulated by these lowest common denominators, and then sell that information to disinterested or even misaligned third-parties.

2. The human being is an irreducibly unique expression of *LoveIntelligence*. And that also has to be cultivated; we have to train ourselves—we discern, and we practice. We're not naturally gorgeous. We are naturally, intrinsically good, but that intrinsic goodness also has to be trained. The nature of the human being, in the deepest understandings of all the great traditions, is that we are born in consciousness, and then we fall away from our awareness that we are consciousness. We fall away from our awareness that we are irreducibly unique expressions of Evolutionary Love. So, if we're untrained, we're driven by our lowest common denominator.

In fact, the intrinsic nature of Cosmos, according to all the interior sciences, as well as our own first-person experience, is that I have to practice and cultivate: *I train, I work out, I exercise my goodness until I become more deep, more good, more true, more beautiful, and more refined.*

All of that is ignored by the view of the human being as solely a social self.

## WHO AM I? THE UNIQUE SELF NARRATIVE

Actually, our interior humanity—our choice, our individuation beyond ego—is not our separate self—but our Unique Self. This is the realization that I'm a *unique* expression of the Field we call True Self.

We say: *I am part of this larger Field of LoveDesire, of Eros, of LoveIntelligence, of consciousness. I'm an irreducibly unique expression of that field*—that's Unique Self.

Now, notice that the Unique Self bypasses the pathologies of the hyper-separate self. The hyper-separate self moves into a hyper-individuality, and the hyper-social self moves into a hyper-collectivism.

**So the social self ignores the separate self, the individuated human being, and the individuated human being ignores the social self. Both of them get lost.**

## SOCIAL SELF: RATS IN THE MAZE OF THE TECH PLEX

There's a direct line from Skinner to Facebook. Facebook says: *Everyone has a desire to express themselves, we're going to connect everyone, and they're going to share about their lives.*

Facebook is expressing, in these banal terms, the original vision of B.F. Skinner—and through his successor, Alex Pentland at the MIT Media Lab: to control society through avoiding risk by removing uniqueness and anomaly and being able to nudge and direct people, through social pressure, to behave appropriately with the herd.

That's insanely insidious. It underlies the agendas of Google and Facebook. When Google says they want to "organize the world's information"— for Google, information is everything, that's tech-speak; **for Google, information is Reality**—Google actually is saying *I want to organize Reality*.

Sergey Brin, and Larry Page, and Mark Zuckerberg say: "Our goal is the societal goal." The "societal goal" of herding humanity into this larger social self in which free will has disappeared—as Pentland says explicitly, as Skinner said explicitly—in which the autonomous human has disappeared, in which interiority doesn't matter.

Skinner and Pentland both note explicitly: *Interiority doesn't matter. We gather information about the nature of human social interaction.*

**We create artificial groups of human beings who can be manipulated by mathematically derived algorithms that say, "If you see this, this, and this in a particular order"**—*an advertisement for socks, followed by a four-second gap in which you see a picture of three kittens, and you see then a third image of a woman dressed in a particular way—and if you run them in that particular order—and it's been split-tested through Facebook a billion times*—**"there's a particular group of people who will respond in a particular way to the next offer that follows."**

Essentially, what's happening is that the social self is not the social self who's intimately connected and part of the Intimate Universe. The social self is the one who's put into an artificial data group that figures out what your lowest common denominator, reflexive reaction will be to a series of stimuli, literally like a rat in a maze. We are the rats in the maze of the tech plex, which has reduced the human being—in B.F. Skinner's phrase—to a *manipulable social self*.

No, that's not right. We are not only social selves, and nor are we merely separate selves. **Rather, in Unique Self, the highest version of social self, my natural, individuated participation in the Field of LoveDesire and the Field of Intimacy is integrated.**

## UNIQUE SELF AS PART OF A SYMPHONY

Separate self points to Unique Self because separate self talks about my higher individuation beyond separation. And Unique Self also picks up deeply on social self, but in its highest form, which is that we're actually affected by each other because we live in an Intimate Universe.

We're part of the same Field of *Amor*; we're part of the same Field of Desire; we're part of the same Field of Love—which is why Alex Pentland's mathematical equations even work at all. The reason they work is because we are affected by social pressure.

We are social beings, *but we're unique social beings.*

---

## We're irreducibly unique. We choose and we create, and our interiority is a unique expression of the interior face of the Cosmos.

---

So we're not merely social selves, and we're not merely separate selves. Social self and separate self can actually rise beyond skin-encapsulated egos, beyond lowest-common-denominator, manipulable human beings; social self and separate self rise into True Self. True Self is the One Field, the One Heart, the One Desire, the One Breath, the One World, the One Evolution.

The total number of True Selves in the world is one. Every single one of us participates in that same True Self.

And then we rise, we deepen, and we realize we're not just fused in True Self; we are irreducibly unique expressions of the *LoveIntelligence* and *LoveBeauty* of the Cosmos.

- *Who are you?* You are a unique chapter and verse in the Amorous Cosmos.
- *Who are you?* You are a unique chapter and verse in The Universe: A Love Story.
- *Who are you?* The trajectory of your Unique Self is the next stage of evolution itself.
- *Who are you?* You're an irreducibly unique expression of the *LoveIntelligence* and *LoveBeauty* that's the initiating and animating Eros, desire, and intelligence of All-That-Is, that lives in you, as you, and through you, that never was, is, or will be ever again—other than through you.

As such, you're not merely social self, and you're not merely separate self. You are Unique Self, and you can turn to your unique circle of intimacy and influence, to which you are allured and which is allured to you—which is the intention of Cosmos.

Cosmos is not random in any essential sense; randomness always appears as part of a larger order, a larger elegance, a larger vector, a larger direction, and a larger *telos*.

Cosmos has direction.

It moves from mud to Mozart, from bacteria to Bach, from dirt to Shakespeare. It moves from matter, to life, to mind, through all of the individuated levels at each of those three great stages. And all of that pours into you—the irreducibly unique set of allurements configured by Cosmos—so that you may give your Unique Gift to your unique circle of intimacy and influence.

- Are you a social self? Well, of course you are. That's true but partial. You're part of this larger social whole. "It's not good to be lonely." Our interior seeks other interiors.
- Are you a separate self? Of course you're, in some sense, separate and individuated. That's true but partial.
- Ultimately, there is no separation. Ultimately, we're part of One Field.
- We're individuated expressions of that Field, with our unique gorgeousness and unique beauty that is the intention of All-That-Is.

And then we come together in Unique Self Symphonies; we come together as part of a Planetary Awakening in Love through Unique Self Symphonies. That's not a social hive in which you're reduced and manipulated. It's not a superorganism in which a degraded version of you is controlled by upgraded algorithms.

> *It's a Planetary Awakening in Outrageous Love and Eros through the irreducibly unique Eros that lives in you as you play your Unique Self instrument in the larger Unique Self Symphony.*

Oh my Goddess!

Yes, that's what we're here to do.

# CHAPTER TWELVE

# THE GOOD NEWS: HOMO AMOR, WE ARE ALL NEEDED

*Episode 233 — March 28, 2021*

## THE DANGERS OF INACCURATE, PARTIAL STORIES

We are here in this moment in history, in this time between worlds, in this time between stories, to tell the new story, to stand for the Story of the Intimate Universe. It's not just another story or fanciful conjecture but the deepest nature of Reality as we know it today, based on the highest integration available to us of the interior sciences, the exterior sciences, the validated insights from premodern, modern, and postmodern thought, woven together in a larger whole greater than the sum of the parts.

That is the new story, the only genuine human response to the potential of catastrophic risk that we've seen, in small part, during the pandemic, when we realized "it wasn't too big to fail," and to the more profound threat—which wipes out all of the future—of existential risk.

The most important response to existential and catastrophic risk is the telling of a new story because **the generator function, the root cause of existential and catastrophic risk, is a failure of Story**. It's a story about the human being, about human identity:

- It's a story about the "we," about human community.
- It's a story about power.

- It's a story about desire.

Most stories claim to be whole when at best they're only partial. **To the precise extent that a story about Reality**—that our universe story, our narrative of identity, our narrative of community, our narrative of power, our narrative of desire—**is inaccurate, that it overclaims, that it leaves important things out of the picture, those externalities undermine the structure of society.**

The generator function of existential risk is this failure of Story. For example, the story of modernity gives us a great gift in that it sees, importantly, the centrality of the individual in a way that premodernity never could. Yet its pathology is that it sees the individual as a separate self who's ultimately alienated from the larger whole, and it also disqualifies the Universe. It takes the Universe out of the Tao, out of intrinsic Value, out of its intrinsic wholeness, out of its intrinsic, awe-inspiring, reverent nature. **We step out of the Tao, or appear to.**

And then we begin to take partial stories; we take bits of the sciences, and we weave them into a false whole, which is a reductionist, materialist view of Reality in which the human being is but a separate self.

The human being gains value and status through their participation in a success story, which is about production and commodification, and is governed by win/lose metrics. That win/lose metric success story—that story of modernity which apotheosizes the individual—brought great dignity to the world:

- It brought universal human rights.
- It brought third-person science.
- It brought modern medicine.
- It brought an explosion of life on the planet.

**But it also brought great pathologies**—not just the dignities of modernity but modernity's disasters—**which have marched us right up to the precipice itself**, to the potential eleventh hour of human history, to the potential death of the future, the potential death of our humanity, which is what we call "existential risk" and "catastrophic risk."

## RECLAIMING THE EVANGELICAL SPARK THAT HAS BEEN HIJACKED

*What does it mean to be an evangelical, for real?*

I spent three years out of the teaching world where I worked in a high-tech, entrepreneurial setting, working for a company that bought start-ups. I wanted to know what the world looked like not from the perspective of the teacher, so I entered the business world just to feel the real world. When I would go to Infinity Loop, to Cupertino, to Silicon Valley, and had all sorts of meetings with people, their cards always said, "evangelist": "Apple evangelists," "Macintosh evangelists," etc. We need to reclaim that word. Evangelist means that we're sharing the good news, and we're excited about the good news. That's a big deal.

**We get to be excited about the good news.**

Because the good news is simple: we realize that there's a choice in the world, and the choice is simple. We can choose to be in the Tao—and to be in the Tao means we're within meaning, within Value: **The world has a plenitude of meaning and a plenitude of Value.** All the stories we tell about it are important and sacred because, ultimately, there's an irreducible Value underneath everything: *an irreducible Goodness, an irreducible Truth, an irreducible Beauty.*

*There are only two choices in the world: either everything is meaningful or nothing is meaningful.*

Either I live in the Tao, or I have the illusion that I'm outside of the Tao—and that difference is everything. That's the whole story.

So the word "evangelical" has been hijacked. We can't allow its hijacking to turn us into tepid, disinterested, semi-intellectual posturers who are talking about things only from this third-person distance as if it was just an intellectual conversation. No. The very One Heart, the very One Breath of Reality is at stake.

The future's at stake.

Do we live in the Tao, in which every human being has irreducible uniqueness and irreducible value, in which *life itself is part of the overriding and overarching wholeness that inspires us to awe, to reverence, to service, to delight, and to joy*? Or did Shakespeare get it right in *Macbeth*: "Tomorrow, and tomorrow, and tomorrow creeps in this petty pace, day after day, to the last syllable of recorded time. Life is nothing but a tale told by an idiot, full of sound and fury, signifying nothing." **Those are the choices.**

*A tale told by an idiot, full of sound and fury, signifying nothing*—we know that's not true because "anthro-ontologically," in our own first-person experience, we feel goodness, we feel truth, and we feel beauty—and we know that it matters.

If anything matters, then everything matters.

*I'm either in the Tao, or I'm outside of the Tao.*

That's good news. We're excited about that good news, and we're not embarrassed to be excited about that good news. **We're not ashamed of being evangelists.** Steve Jobs was not ashamed to be an evangelist, and all he was showing was an elegant operating system. So we have to wrest the hijackers' grip from the term "evangelical."

Of course, the term "evangelical" can be hijacked, and we have to reject the hijacking. The term "evangelical" can be hijacked by people who say, *We're going to induce a state experience, of a kind of euphoria, that we're going to use to transmit fear:*

- Fear of hell.

- Fear of your own body.
- Fear of all that stands against you.

*Your body stands against you, your fallenness stands against you, your lack of grace stands against you. We're going to whip you up to some state of fervor—which is called "evangelical fervor," but it's a hijacking of the term—and we're going to download fear into your body. We're going to use that state for all manner of abuse: intellectual abuse, moral abuse, and spiritual abuse.*

**That's not the "evangelical" we're talking about—that's a hijacking of the good news.** That frame of an "evangelical" that we often associate it with—whether it's a New Age evangelical or a fundamentalist evangelical in one of the religions—where we say:

*We've got radical certitude, and we're the only people who have access to the truth.*

*We're going to whip you up to a frenzy until you step into our version of the truth, and if you don't, you're somehow damned, you're shunned.* This might be a materialist scientific shunning, a New Age shunning, an Integral shunning, a Catholic shunning, a Jewish shunning, an Islamic shunning, a Confucian shunning, or a Tibetan Buddhist shunning—all of which have their own versions of shunning the outsider who doesn't step into their version of the good news.

That's not being an evangelical—**to be an evangelist is to be an Outrageous Lover.**

## TO BE AN EVANGELIST IS TO BE AN OUTRAGEOUS LOVER

Being an evangelical means that we enter into ecstatic states. Higher states of consciousness are utterly essential, and ecstatic technologies are critical. All genuine human *gnosis* is based on ecstatic technologies of various forms: contemplative technologies, pharmacological technologies, intellectual technologies, mystical technologies, ethical technologies, embodied technologies.

Ecstatic technologies are critical. They open us up to not just higher states of consciousness but to higher *structure stages* of consciousness:

We can reach cosmocentric consciousness, meaning we have a felt sense of love, care, and concern:

- Not just for myself and my survival, my people, which is the general state of most of the liberal community in the world.
- Not just to myself and my country, my survival, people in my country and my religion, which is the state of most of the conservative community in the world
- Not just even to all human beings.

Cosmocentric consciousness means I have a felt sense of love, care, and concern for every human being. I'm madly in love with Reality itself:

- I'm madly in love with love itself.
- I'm lived as love.
- I feel the dolphins.
- I speak to the pandas.
- I dance with wolves.
- I open up to extra-terrestrials and extra-dimensionals, other frames of being and anomalous experiences—because I'm madly in love with Reality.

I move from being "Homo armor," the armored evangelical who's pretending to share the good news but is actually sharing the bad news.

- I'm armored.
- I'm constricted. My body is somehow of the devil.
- I'm the only one with the truth. No one else has it.
- I think I'm telling you the good news, but I'm giving you the worst news in the world.

## HOMO AMOR, WE ARE ALL NEEDED

**We have to move from Homo armor to *Homo amor*.**

---

*We're all irreducibly unique expressions of the LoveIntelligence of Cosmos. We're all desperately needed by All-That-Is. We're all intended, desired, chosen, needed, loved, adored. That's the intrinsic nature of being an Evolutionary Unique Self.*

---

That's the good news. We are wildly excited about that, we are passionate about that, and we will not apologize for our passion because it's only that passion that will address suffering. It's only that passion that will address two billion people on the planet who don't have sanitation or drinking water—because somehow we cut those people out of our lives as we're so busily self-involved.

**We got to be madly passionate. We've got to be Outrageous Lovers.** I remember, with Kristina Kincaid when we were deep in the early *dharma* of Outrageous Love back in 2012 and 2013, and we wanted to take out the first Outrageous Love.com site. Kristina mocked up that first site and created this gorgeous, aesthetic, holy place. We looked online to see if anyone else used the term "Outrageous Love" and saw that the only other people to have used it were Christian evangelical communities. Mad blessings to those communities, but they weren't saying what we were saying. They got the sense of Outrageous Love, but it meant *Outrageous Love only if you understand, like we do, our particular understanding of the exclusivity of Jesus's message. And you need to have a particular kind of faith in Jesus*—which excluded anyone who didn't belong to that particular brand of Pentecostal, evangelical Christianity.

That's not what Outrageous Love means at all.

That's ordinary, egoic, constricted, ethnocentric consciousness.

# THE EXISTENTIAL RISK OF TECHNOLOGY

We need to actually make Outrageous Love genuinely outrageous. It's not just unlimited love, it's *outrageous*.

## OUTRAGEOUS LOVE: WE'RE OUTRAGED

Outrageous contains the word rage in it:

- I'm outraged at anything that's small and contracted.
- I'm outraged that two billion people don't have access to drinking water.
- I'm outraged that there are child soldiers in the Congo.
- I'm outraged about the fire that just took place in Bangladesh that could have been stopped and is not being dealt with.
- I'm outraged that there are AK-47 guns all available across much of the Western world—and particularly the United States when there's no reason those guns should be available. And it's got nothing to do with politics.

**We're outraged. And we're filled with the outrageous joy of knowing who we are.** We don't have all the details worked out. All models are limited.

The Tao is underneath the 10,000 things. I was talking about four or five weeks ago to my friend Daniel about the Tao.

*The Tao means we're inside of Outrageous Love. We fall on our faces in rapture and reverence, and we stand tall, proud, audacious, and dignified as irreducibly Unique Selves joining hands, each of us expressions of the Tao. A Unique Self is the Tao in person as you.*

Our intention is that we are a band of Outrageous Lovers: excited, passionate, outraged, standing at this moment in this time between worlds, in the time between stories, standing in this eleventh hour and saying:

*We're going to give everything to tell this new story in which everyone has a place. To articulate a universal grammar of value that can become the matrix of a new story, which is the plotline of a global ethos for a global civilization.*

That's our intention. We're evangelicals all the way.

We're sharing the good news—and there are lots of ways we can share it. We need a podcast, we need festivals and *dharma* labs, and we need study groups—we need all sorts of forums. We're not embarrassed about it. We're not ashamed by it.

- We are privileged by our passion.
- We are boldly, amazingly, and radically humbled by our own ability to share this news.
- We share it every day, every hour with ourselves. Passion waxes and wanes. We re-choose again.
- We choose joy, we choose the new story, and we choose to respond to history, which desperately needs all of us together.

## EVOLUTIONARY LOVE CODE: FOR TRUE EVANGELISM, WE NEED BOTH ECSTATIC STATES AND DEVELOPMENTAL STAGES

We need to be evangelicals.

Evangelicals are bearers of the good news.

For true evangelicals, however, the good news includes everyone and everything.

No one is left out of this circle of Eros.

For true evangelism, we need ecstatic states and developmental stages mediated through *dharma*, or what we call First Principles and First Values.

# THE EXISTENTIAL RISK OF TECHNOLOGY

The paradox of evangelicals today, whether it's New Age evangelicals or political evangelicals, is it has become associated with polarity: *we're in and you're out*—but that's the opposite of Eros.

**You only need to place someone outside the circle when you actually don't experience the good news, when you don't experience yourself inside the circle, when you don't have the knowing, the awareness, when the Tao is not awake in you.**

You feel small and contracted. You desperately—I desperately, we desperately—want to be inside the circle, so we place everybody else outside the circle *to give ourselves the illusion that we're on the inside.*

That's not Eros. The evangelical is erotic for true evangelicals.

Back to the code: *For true evangelicals, the good news includes everyone and everything. No one is left out of the circle of Eros. For true evangelism, we need ecstatic states and developmental stages*—*Wake up and grow up*, as John Welwood wrote so beautifully.

I've got to be not just egocentric, not just ethnocentric, and not just worldcentric, but cosmocentric. And it has to be *mediated through a dharma, through First Principles and First Values.*

I'm reading a book that a colleague of mine wrote about ecstatic technologies. He writes proudly about how Silicon Valley, Navy SEALs, and maverick scientists are stripping away the spiritual content, hacking the great traditions, and accessing ecstatic technologies. The entire book is about how wonderful that is. However:

*You don't want ecstatic states without developmental stages, without dharma, without spiritual content—or else it actually does become dangerous.*

Just like the evangelicals of the old churches became dangerous. They were telling a story that defaced the human dignity of everyone outside of their circle. So too, contemporary tech evangelicals, who are hacking ecstatic states, "stealing fire" in order to perpetrate on society the control of a tech elite, a kind of TechnoFeudalism—that's equally dangerous.

So Apple evangelicals or Google evangelicals or Facebook evangelicals are, in their own way, as profoundly dangerous because they're driven by a very small elite with a hidden profit motive, with a hidden lining of intense greed, just like the churches often tragically had.

They're foisting upon society *upgraded algorithms and downgraded human beings*.

We have to be wary of misguided evangelicals.

At the same time, we can't give up our passion. We have to claim the evangelical mantle not only for ourselves but for anyone and everyone who wants to get involved in telling the new story—in a way in which everyone's inside the circle, in a way that integrates the most validated and important insights from all streams of wisdom—premodern, modern, and postmodern—into a genuine new whole greater than the sum of the parts.

**We need to tell a new story that stands against suffering, that stands against contraction, that stands against those limiting beliefs that keep us small in the world, and that stands against the win/lose metrics that is the generator function for existential and catastrophic risk.**

## IN EVERY GREAT TRADITION THERE'S AN INTIMATE INCARNATION OF THE DIVINE

We need to integrate the best of evolutionary science: the best of superstring theory, the best of molecular biology, the best of horizontal gene transfer, and the best of symbiogenesis; **we need to integrate all of the sciences with the best of the most critical validated insights of the great traditions.**

We're used to thinking that what's important about the great religions is their shared universal truths—that's true. For example, the perennial philosophy, at its best, is about the underlying shared truths of the great traditions. It's often termed by perennial philosophers, including my friend Ken, as *extrapolating the general principles of shared truth from the particular settings.*

There's great truth in that, but we need to go a step further. The traditions of the great religions are not just surface structures. There are some that are social constructions of Reality that are surface structures, but often that's not the case.

> *Just like there's a unique love language between beloveds, so at the height, in the depth, in the authentic essence of every great tradition, there's an intimate language of the finite and the Infinite. There's an intimate incarnation of the Tao. There's an intimate incarnation of Eros.*

So, for example, Catholicism has many sins, as does Islam, as does Judaism, as does Buddhism, but they also each have greatness. It's not just that the religions were disasters. The religions were expressions of a premodern world, and in the premodern world governance was a disaster.

**The flaws of the religions are not particular religious flaws; they're flaws of the structure of consciousness that dominated at the time. Those flaws, for the most part, existed in every part of society, not just religion.** It's not like you had these beautiful, gorgeous, beneficent monarchies with ugly religions. No. You had ugly expressions of power, both in religion and governance.

However, at their best, in their esoteric cores and in their most pure and beautiful teachings, **each of the great traditions contains an intimate language**.

Each religion has a Unique Self.

That Unique Self is not just a surface structure; it is a depth structure.

It's a uniquely irreducibly intimate language of Spirit.

## PASSOVER: RECLAIMING THE BROKEN PART

In the Hebrew wisdom tradition of Passover there are *Seders*, a ritual re-enactment of the exodus from Egypt. And in the *Seders*, there are three *matzahs*. I just want to share with you one dimension of the practice where you break the middle matzah in two, and you take this broken piece of matzah, and you wrap it in a cloth, and you hide it. Then, this middle matzah is searched for by the children in the home, and when it's found, the children often negotiate with the parents or the caretakers for a prize for finding it.

So what's at the core of this tradition, which lies at the very heart of the Seder?

> *All of us, at some point, broke.*
> *Something broke inside of us.*

What happened is that we split off; we broke off a part of ourselves.

**That emergent adult in us went and hid that broken part. And we hid it so well that we ourselves couldn't even find it.** We broke off a piece of our story, and we couldn't access it anymore.

*Pesach*, "Passover" in Hebrew, in mysticism is *Peh Sach*: "The mouth that speaks." In the lineage, the practice of the day is to tell the story of leaving Egypt.

**But Egypt is not just a historical place.** In the interior tradition, "Egypt," in Hebrew, is *Mitzrayim*. *Mitzrayim* means "the narrow place." Egypt is the narrow place, the place which in the body is the throat—because mystically, every nation mentioned in the sacred text represents a different part of the body.

**Egypt is the narrow place, the throat.**

It's the place where:

- I couldn't tell my story, I couldn't give my all, I couldn't be my all.
- So I contracted, made myself smaller, and split off a piece of myself.

*I am the matzah*—which is where the tradition came later in Christianity: *I am the wafer.*

- I am the body of the Divine. I am an irreducible Unique Self.
- I've split off a part of myself, and I've hidden it.

*I've split off a part of my dreams, and I don't believe that those dreams belong in an adult world; I don't believe that those dreams belong in a mature and settled human being, so I split off that part of me.*

- It's hidden.
- It's so hidden that I can't even find it myself.
- It's so hidden that I've forgotten about it, but not only have I forgotten, *I've forgotten that I forgot.*

**Not only is it hidden, but it's hidden so well that even its hiddenness is hidden.** It's an incredibly sacred text: *Haster astir panai*, "I will hide, I will hide my face"—and *panai* means my interiority, my dreams, my deepest inner dream and longing and yearning. So the mystics ask, *Why does the text say, "I will hide, I will hide" in a language of double?* **Because it's a double hiding.**

*The hiddenness itself is hidden.*

The Hebrew word for "world" is *olam*, which means hidden; the world is a place of hiding. It's a place of broken hearts and broken vessels. Hemingway reminds us: *the world breaks all of us.*

**We're all broken in some way. But, in the end, that breaking is not a bug in the system; it's a feature.**

---

## *There's nothing more whole than a broken heart.*

---

A version of Passover was the Last Supper. You don't need to be part of the tradition; you can learn this particular intimate language. On Passover, we say:

- For the first time, I'm going to find that hidden dream.
- I'm going to reclaim that broken part.
- I'm going to know that I can be a powerful, developed, mature adult—and dream my dream.
- I'm going to know that I can speak my passion and feel the potency and power of my passion, that my passion is good.
- I'm going to know that my dream is my evangelical message; it's my good news that I have to share with the world.

So who's ready, my friends, in this moment, to find the broken piece of matzah? Who's ready to reclaim the dream? That's what it means to be an Outrageous Lover. An Outrageous Lover means *I outrageously love Reality; I commit Outrageous Acts of Love.*

It always has to begin with:

*I outrageously love myself and outrageously love my dreams.*

Then I can outrageously love you, and I can outrageously love we, and I can outrageously love Reality. We can dream together, and we can make those dreams real.

It's ours. We're a band of Outrageous Lovers. We're dreaming the dream. *What happens to a dream deferred,* wrote Langston Hughes, *does it dry up like a raisin in the sun?*

When we defer the dream, we become corrupt, and we dry up like a raisin in the sun.

- Let's dare to dream the dream.
- Let's dare to be evangelicals.
- Let's dare to stand on the brink, to stand in this abyss at this time between worlds and time between stories and be Outrageous Lovers.
- Let's dare to speak into the darkness and say, *Let there be light.*

We are the light.

*For with you is the source of light; in your light, we see light.*

# INDEX

*Adonai Eloheinu* 167
allurement 105, 115, 117, 118, 119, 122, 123, 124, 129, 135, 136, 165, 166
American Revolution 138, 151, 152
Amorous Cosmos 49, 50, 97, 98, 114, 117, 129, 168, 179, 190
Anthro-Ontology 75, 98
St. Thomas Aquinas 44
Ark of the Covenant 122, 136, 155, 156, 157
artificial intelligence 7, 8, 9, 14, 51, 59, 75, 76
attachment theory 135
attention 8, 10, 11, 18, 19, 45, 50, 58, 62, 63, 65, 87, 170, 171
  the hijacking of 8, 10, 45, 49, 50, 71, 131, 150, 170, 195, 196, 197
Auden, W.H 19

Baal Shem Tov 133, 135
Beethoven 21
being and becoming 3, 74
*Beyond Freedom and Dignity*
  (Skinner) 31, 34, 36, 38, 41, 69
Big Bang 162
biometric sensors 16, 17, 48, 62, 63
Bloom, Howard 39
Brin, Sergey 12, 15, 23, 44, 50, 188
Brown, Brené 30
Buddha 34, 37
Buddhism 34, 37, 197

Carr, Nicolas 169, 170, 182
*Cast Away* (movie) 99, 110
Chomsky, Noam 31, 32
Christianity 36, 44, 199, 206
Cohen, Leonard 86, 102, 156, 168, 183
Communism 44, 91
cosmocentric consciousness 91, 198
CosmoErotic Universe 105, 179

Darwin, Charles 67
da Vinci, Leonardo 55, 67, 69, 169, 177
death of humanity 26, 35, 80, 81, 93, 94, 112, 113, 140, 151
death of our humanity 26, 35, 37, 61, 81, 89, 94, 113, 140, 145, 151, 195
deconstruction 5, 48
deepest heart's desire 28, 86, 107, 109, 140
democracy 8, 9, 10, 47, 48, 184
depth structures 2, 5
digital assistants 17, 62, 71
digital dictatorship 48, 50
digital intimacy 25, 50, 81, 82
DNA 165
dystopia 1, 16, 56, 82, 103, 106, 112, 179

*Enlightenment Now* (Pinker) 112
Eros
  the sexual as model of 136

# INDEX

evangelism  129, 195, 196, 197, 198, 199, 202, 203, 207
evolution  3, 8, 18, 19, 28, 43, 49, 52, 53, 57, 60, 83, 96, 100, 105, 106, 107, 108, 116, 125, 126, 129, 130, 131, 137, 138, 142, 145, 152, 153, 160, 162, 163, 177, 181, 182, 183, 190
  in person  162, 163
*Evolution 2.0* (Marshall)  116
Evolutionary Family  106, 131
evolutionary impulse  3, 28, 57, 70, 79, 131, 150, 163, 172
Evolutionary Love  50, 70, 80, 81, 82, 89, 108, 126, 152, 169, 170, 187
evolutionary psychology  177
Evolutionary Unique Self  31, 49, 80, 176, 199
evolution of value  146
existentialism  40
existential risk  15, 26, 33, 34, 35, 36, 37, 38, 40, 41, 49, 52, 53, 58, 59, 60, 61, 65, 66, 75, 80, 81, 82, 87, 92, 93, 94, 103, 112, 113, 137, 140, 151, 164, 193, 194, 195

feminine  3, 125, 178
Feuerbach, Ludwig  128
Field of Consciousness  27, 29, 45, 74, 88, 184
Field of Intimacy  85, 101, 166
Field of Personhood  99, 101
finitude  21
First Principles and First Values  1, 2, 9, 11, 12, 15, 18, 19, 20, 21, 50, 52, 53, 55, 60, 68, 69, 70, 91, 92, 94, 98, 99, 100, 109, 113, 177, 202
Foucault, Michel  5
French Revolution  138, 151
Freud, Sigmund  67, 164
Future of Humanity Institute  59

global intimacy disorder  87, 113, 153, 164
God  26, 50, 56, 57, 76, 85, 86, 91, 95, 101, 103, 105, 107, 110, 111, 113, 115, 117, 118, 119, 120, 128, 129, 131, 132, 136, 140, 142, 149, 155, 167, 168, 175, 182, 183, 184
  as the Infinity of Intimacy  75, 85, 86, 101, 102, 109, 111, 118, 119, 131, 132, 142, 143, 144, 157, 166, 167, 168, 182, 183
  as the Infinity of Power  117, 131
  name of  91
Google  6, 7, 9, 12, 13, 16, 17, 22, 23, 32, 39, 42, 43, 47, 50, 51, 54, 65, 66, 68, 72, 87, 188, 203
  six declarations of  12, 13, 17, 42, 153

Hafiz  182
Harari, Yuval  48, 128, 171
Harris, Tristan  11, 19
*haster astir panai* (I will hide my face)  207
holdables  16, 17, 62
*Homo amor*  15, 49, 50, 73, 80, 92, 96, 104, 105, 106, 126, 199
*Homo Deus*  149
*Homo imaginus*  126, 128
Hubbard, Barbara Marx  114
Hughes, Langston  208

imagination
  crisis of  125, 127, 128
Infinite Intimate  85
Infinity of Intimacy  75, 85, 86, 101, 102, 109, 111, 118, 119, 131, 132, 142, 143, 144, 157, 166, 167, 168, 182, 183
interiority  9, 18, 20, 52, 100, 181, 188, 190, 207
interior sciences  45, 72, 83, 91, 107,

114, 115, 147, 166, 187, 193
Internet of Things 16, 17, 62, 63
Intimate Universe 50, 81, 97, 114, 117, 129, 131, 161, 164, 167, 176, 179, 180, 189, 193
Kook, Abraham 172, 173, 174

Lewis, C.S. 34, 35, 36, 37, 38, 40, 43, 44, 47, 48, 52, 69
logical positivism 40
love
  evolution of 8, 53, 106, 107, 129, 137, 138, 152, 160, 162, 183
LoveBeauty 28, 46, 73, 79, 88, 126, 190
LoveIntelligence 28, 46, 73, 74, 75, 79, 88, 119, 126, 143, 187, 188, 190, 199

*Macbeth* (Shakespeare) 196
machine intelligence 7, 8, 14, 29, 42, 47, 51, 54, 63, 64, 65, 70, 71, 81, 84, 181, 185, 186
Mack, John 104
Marshall, Perry 116
Marxism 91, 93
Maslow, Abraham 120
materialism 36, 40, 45, 52, 98, 145, 177, 178, 181, 184, 194, 197
Mead, Margaret 61
Merzenich, Mike 164, 170
modernity 2, 4, 6, 38, 53, 57, 79, 94, 95, 96, 112, 127, 138, 146, 147, 153, 177, 178, 193, 194, 203
Moses 155

Nadella, Satya 84
natural law 1, 2, 3, 4, 5, 6, 11, 35, 43, 44, 52, 54, 55
neo-Darwinism 36, 40
nervous system of the planet 6, 46, 49, 52, 53, 80, 81, 82, 86, 150
neuroscience 83
New Age 66, 67, 90, 95, 107, 127, 138, 197, 202
Nussbaum, Martha 135

*olam* (world) 207
Ord, Toby 112
Outrageous Love 21, 76, 92, 94, 97, 101, 108, 109, 126, 127, 134, 140, 146, 152, 153, 163, 166, 168, 171, 174, 176, 179, 192, 199, 200
Outrageous Love Letters 21

Page, Larry 12, 15, 23, 41, 50, 188
Palace of Thought 173, 174, 175
Passover 205, 206, 207
Patel, Amit 12
Pentland, Alex 39, 41, 43, 44, 45, 46, 47, 48, 49, 52, 64, 65, 66, 67, 68, 69, 70, 72, 74, 75, 86, 185, 186, 188, 189
perennial philosophy 1, 2, 3, 4, 5, 204
personhood 50, 54, 55, 56, 64, 74, 85, 86, 87, 92, 99, 100, 101, 110, 132, 154, 167
Pinker, Steven 112
Planetary Awakening in Love through Unique Self Symphonies 61, 82, 107, 151, 183, 191
Plato 36
polarization 10
postmodernity 1, 4, 5, 6, 48, 49, 52, 53, 54, 57, 79, 94, 95, 107, 127, 130, 138, 146, 147, 152, 153, 171, 193, 203
prayer 3, 21, 76, 82, 83, 85, 86, 98, 99, 100, 101, 102, 111, 116, 117, 119, 131, 133, 140, 143, 155, 167, 168, 179, 180, 182
premodernity 2, 4, 57, 94, 95, 127, 131, 138, 147, 177, 193, 194, 203, 204

Reality
  as Eros 70, 92, 126, 148

re-selfing 87, 88, 97
*reshimu* (traces) 158
Rumi 101, 115, 182
Russell, Bertrand 100

Sartre, J.P. 109, 154
Schmidt, Eric 12
separate self 19, 21, 25, 26, 27, 30, 31, 34, 36, 37, 38, 39, 40, 41, 45, 46, 52, 53, 64, 66, 67, 73, 74, 82, 87, 88, 92, 96, 97, 131, 184, 187, 188, 189, 190, 191, 194
sexuality 3, 4, 5, 124, 136
Shakespeare, William 191, 196
Skinner, B.F. ix, x, 28, 31, 32, 33, 34, 36, 37, 38, 39, 40, 41, 42, 43, 44, 45, 46, 47, 48, 49, 50, 52, 53, 64, 67, 69, 70, 74, 75, 185, 188, 189
social media 10, 23, 32, 42, 58, 66, 70, 71, 150
*Social Physics* (Pentland) 39, 41, 43, 185
social self 25, 26, 27, 28, 31, 36, 37, 40, 41, 42, 45, 46
*Song of Solomon* 107, 136, 179
source code of culture and consciousness 49, 53, 55, 59, 61, 67, 71, 72, 90, 94, 95, 96, 106, 108, 112, 117, 138, 160
Stein, Zak 149
Stevenson, Ian 118
Story of Value 148
success story 5, 6, 12, 15, 16, 23, 38, 80, 92, 194
*sunyata* 167
surface structures 2, 5, 204

Tao, the 35, 36, 40, 43, 44, 47, 68, 69, 70, 72, 86, 137, 140, 141, 142, 143, 144, 145, 146, 147, 148, 151, 152, 154, 155, 157, 158, 159, 161, 163, 167, 168, 169, 170, 172, 173, 175, 178, 194, 195, 196, 200, 201, 202, 204
TechnoFeudalism 149, 186, 203
tech plex 9, 10, 11, 15, 16, 19, 20, 25, 39, 41, 42, 44, 45, 46, 48, 49, 50, 52, 53, 55, 71, 75, 80, 81, 82, 83, 85, 86, 87, 88, 149, 150, 153, 181, 188, 189
*The Abolition of Man* (Lewis) ix, 34, 40
*The Age of Surveillance Capitalism* (Zuboff) 6
*The Body Keeps the Score* (van der Kolk) 83
*The Language of Emotions* (Nussbaum) 135
*The Lucifer Principle* (Bloom) 39
*The Social Dilemma* (movie) 10, 11, 18, 19, 20, 33
True Self 3, 25, 26, 27, 30, 45, 46, 48, 49, 52, 66, 73, 74, 82, 88, 96, 97, 187, 190

Unique Gift 18, 107
Unique Risk 105
Unique Self 12, 15, 18, 19, 23, 25, 26, 27, 28, 29, 30, 31, 33, 37, 46, 48, 49, 50, 52, 53, 55, 61, 66, 72, 73, 74, 76, 78, 79, 80, 82, 87, 88, 89, 90, 96, 97, 103, 107, 108, 118, 131, 147, 148, 149, 150, 151, 153, 154, 168, 176, 183, 187, 188, 189, 190, 191, 192, 199, 200, 205, 206
Unique Self Symphony 15, 23, 30, 31, 55, 66, 72, 73, 76, 79, 80, 87, 88, 96, 147, 148, 149, 150, 154, 168, 192
universal grammar of value 60, 71, 148, 201
universal human rights 8, 194
Universe: A Love Story 49, 114, 123, 165, 190

utopia  1, 56, 82, 103, 104, 105, 106, 112, 179

value
  intrinsic  35, 138, 148, 161, 184
van der Kolk, Bessel  83

*Walden Two* (Skinner)  28, 29, 31, 33, 34, 40, 42, 43, 52
wearables  16, 17, 62
Welwood, John  202
Whitehead, A.N.  100
Wilber, Ken  108, 204
Winnicott, Donald  136

Zuboff, Shoshana  6, 8, 10, 11, 12, 13, 18, 19, 20, 32, 33, 37, 38, 44, 49, 53, 54, 55, 71
Zuckerberg, Mark  15, 23, 41, 44, 188

# VOLUME 18 — The Existential Risk of Technology

## LIST OF EPISODES

1. First Principles 02 — October 10, 2018
2. First Principles 09 — January 31, 2021
3. Episode 222 — January 10, 2021
4. Episode 224 — January 24, 2021
5. Episode 225 — January 31, 2021
6. Episode 226 — February 7, 2021
7. Episode 227 — February 14, 2021
8. Episode 228 — February 21, 2021
9. Episode 230 — March 7, 2021
10. Episode 231 — March 14, 2021
11. Episode 232 — March 21, 2021
12. Episode 233 — March 28, 2021

www.ingramcontent.com/pod-product-compliance
Lightning Source LLC
LaVergne TN
LVHW011151080426
835508LV00007B/343